500
breads

500

breads

the only bread compendium you'll ever need

Carol Beckerman

NEW
HOLLAND

A Quintet Book

First published in Australia in 2013 by
New Holland Publishers (Australia) Pty Ltd
Sydney • Auckland • London • Cape Town

Unit 1, 66 Gibbes Street, Chatswood, NSW 2067 Australia
218 Lake Road, Northcote, Auckland, New Zealand
86 Edgware Road, London W2 2EA, United Kingdom
Wembley Square, First Floor, Solan Road Gardens, Cape Town 8001, South Africa

www.newholland.com.au

ISBN: 978-1-7425-7447-9
QTT.FBRE

This book was conceived, designed and produced by
Quintet Publishing Limited
6 Blundell Street
London N7 9BH
United Kingdom

Food Stylist: Lucy Heeley
Photographer: Ian Garlick
Designer: Jacqui Caulton
Art Director: Michael Charles
Managing Editor: Emma Bastow
Publisher: Mark Searle

10 9 8 7 6 5 4 3 2 1

Printed in China by 1010 Printing International Ltd.

contents

introduction

One of the joys of making your own bread is the smell. It fills every corner of your home, putting smiles on the faces of family and friends, and freshly torn chunks of bread, still warm from the oven, in their hands. In life, there is no greater pleasure.

Bread dough is like a good friend. It is kind and forgiving, patient and flexible, tolerant of beginners and mistakes. Reading too much about yeast and baking bread will intimidate you and put you off even trying. The best technique for learning is to get stuck in it, and after only a couple of practise runs, you will begin to get a feel for the way the yeast reacts, and how the dough develops and grows. It's very easy to over-think it, but remember, people have been doing this for thousands of years...it's not that difficult.

Baking your own bread is a simple pleasure, with ample rewards that easily equal the little amount of effort involved. When most food production has been relegated to the mechanised convenience of hyper-efficient factory production, the skill of baking with yeast is in danger of becoming a lost art. But it is healthy, fun, cheap and delicious – and much easier than you think. There is a therapeutic, almost childlike satisfaction in seeing the results of just six ingredients, in your hands, miraculously transform into a delightful combination of texture and taste, seemingly from nowhere.

a short history
The Hungarians have a saying: 'Bread is older than man'. More than 10,000 years ago, the production of bread led man to live in communities cultivating fields and grain, rather than in isolation, hunting and herding cattle. When he discovered the benefits of growing wheat and barley, the new Stone Age and a farming culture evolved. Ancient man realised that this was a food that he could store, and one that would sustain him through the winter, leaving

him time to develop other skills. At first, preparing the grain and making bread was women's work, but in time, bakeries were formed and the profession of baker became one of the most valued in the community.

Man also realised bread was one of the best foods to sustain a fast-growing population, so the practice spread, and he invented the tools of the trade. He developed the mills and millstones required to grind flour, and built the engines to cultivate vast swathes of land for the large-scale production of cereals. From a beginning of basic unleavened bread cooked on an open fire, we now have specialist, highly appreciated artisan bakers, making complicated combinations of sophisticated flavours.

benefits of baking your own bread

The bread baked in your own kitchen has many benefits over modern factory-produced supermarket bread. It tastes better, reduces the intake of preservatives, is more nutritious and is often substantially cheaper.

The large-scale production of bread today is a balancing act. On one hand, the manufacturers want to produce an edible loaf, and on the other, they want to maximise profit. They want to make a loaf of bread as cheaply as possible, and the result is that they often abandon flavour and nutrition along the way. The manufacturers want to prolong shelf life, so they pack the bread with preservatives and salt to ensure that this is the case. Check the ingredients on a normal supermarket loaf and you will see a substantial list, some of which you will never have heard of, let alone be able to pronounce. You will need just six if you make the bread yourself: flour, yeast, sugar, fat, water and salt.

After a hard day, or even before one, the kneading of a batch of bread dough is calming and therapeutic. It gives a good upper-body workout, exercises the fingers and joints and brings joy to the faces around you.

ingredients

As mentioned, just six ingredients will get you started. An amazing number of recipes are based on bread dough. From pizza to panettone, and brioche to banana bread, the majority of them are based on those six ingredients and a very basic mixing method. You can tweak the basic ingredients to vary the texture and taste in an infinite number of ways, but they all start from the basic six.

flour

Barley, millet, oats, rye and wheat have all been milled for thousands of years in Europe and Asia, and corn was a grain of the Americas. Only wheat – and, to a lesser degree, rye – has the gluten content necessary to make leavened bread. All other flours should be used, in varying combinations, with wheat flour.

Most of the bread dough in this book is made with white (wheat) bread flour, which is 'strong' flour and has a higher protein content than plain flour. This means it has more than 12 per cent protein, and the protein level is an indication of the gluten content, which is what binds the bread together.

To change the taste and texture of the bread, you can incorporate a percentage of other flours, and experimenting to suit your own personal taste is all part of the fun.

Find a good-quality white bread flour that you like as a base, as it is the easiest to work with, and stick with it. The recipes are accurate in this book, but there are lots of factors that play a part in making bread. The humidity, temperature, altitude and the amount of protein in your particular brand will all affect the amount of moisture that the flour will absorb. For that reason, the recipes state that you should check for the feel of the dough and adjust the ratio of liquid and flour, depending upon how sticky or dry the dough feels. After only a couple of recipes, you will begin to get a feel for the dough and will instinctively know whether it needs more water or more flour.

yeast
Yeast is a living organism, and there are three types that you can use for bread making. The first is fresh yeast, which, although it gives a lovely flavour, can be hard to find. If you can obtain it, mix it with a little tepid water to make a paste, which you then add to the flour.

The second is active dry yeast, which mostly needs to be awakened with a shot of sugar and a bath of warm water. The water should be about 43°C (110°F). If it is colder, the yeast will not wake up, and if it is hotter, the yeast will be killed off. I don't bother to check the temperature; if it feels nice and warm, I know it is about right. I like to use this kind of yeast. I like the way the water bubbles as the yeast ferments; this process looks like the beginning of an adventure to me. Most of the recipes in this book contain at least 1 teaspoon of sugar for the yeast to feed on, but it will also feed on flour, but more slowly.

The third type is instant yeast, sometimes called fast-action, and can be used right in the flour without needing a wake-up call. It can, however, be killed by salt, so don't let them fight – add them separately, on different sides of the bowl.

sugar
Yeast ferments best when fed on sugar, which works as a preservative and also helps give a lovely golden colour to the crust. Too much sugar will interfere with the rising action of the yeast and may cause the bread to collapse. Bread and rolls generally are not very sweet anyway, and dessert breads often get their sweetness from a glaze or dry sugar topping.

fat

Fats added to bread will inhibit the formation of gluten, and for this reason, you should use them sparingly. They can, however, be important as they act as a preservative and give a tender, softer texture to the dough. Whether you use butter or oil is a personal preference. I like to use olive oil, especially in Mediterranean recipes, as it keeps the recipe heart-friendly and dairy-free, but softened butter works well in white bread. Stronger-tasting oils, such as sesame or walnut oil, should only be used when they will contribute to the flavour of stronger-tasting ingredients, such as olives or sundried tomatoes. I also sometimes use white vegetable fat, which gives a slightly flakier texture and crustier finish, but I avoid margarine as it usually contains water and will affect the ratio of fluid to flour.

Use just a smear of oil to grease baking tins or use butter. Margarine may cause the bread to scorch.

If you want to cut all fat out of your bread, you could substitute apple sauce or puréed prunes, but as they contain liquid, adjust the amount of water or milk you add to the recipe accordingly.

water

Ordinary tap water is fine for baking bread, but the temperature of the water is worth talking about. All the recipes in this book call for water at a temperature of about 43°C (110°F), as mentioned earlier. This helps promote a speedy rise for the dough, and the speed of this fermentation process is balanced nicely with the flavour of the bread. As you get more experienced at bread making, you can slow down the fermentation process by using cool water. The longer time taken to prove (rise) the bread, the better the flavour, which is why sourdough has a rich and tangy taste – it takes time to mature. If you add milk, however, warm it first, as the fat content will impede the yeast action. Think of the amount of water listed in each recipe as a guide. As mentioned earlier, different flours and different conditions will vary the amount of water absorbed. I think it is better to have a dough that is slightly too wet rather than a dough that is slightly too dry.

salt
Salt is very important in bread. It strengthens the gluten and keeps the bread from tasting bland. Too much, however, will inhibit the action of the yeast. Ordinary cooking salt is fine for adding to bread dough, but coarser flaked sea salt is ideal for adding to the top of bread such as focaccia.

equipment
There are many tools that you could implement in baking bread in your own kitchen, but just a few are essential:

oven
baking sheets and baking tins
bread tins, 450 g (1 lb) and 900 g (1 lb) sizes
lining paper
cling film and plastic bags
dough scraper
water spray
large bowl
large sharp knife
colander with a kitchen towel to use as a
  proving basket

useful but not essential tools:

proving basket
proving cloth
baker's peel
pizza stone
electric stand mixer with a dough
  hook attachment

techniques

mixing the dough

If you are Italian, you will probably do this on a lightly floured work surface, but I prefer to do it in a bowl. Pile the flour and salt into a large bowl, and make a well in the centre. Add the oil or butter to the middle, and pour in most of the yeast liquid. With a fork and a circular movement, gradually incorporate the dry flour from the inner edge of the well and mix into the liquid, continuing until you have used all the flour, and all the liquid if needed. When the dough comes together and becomes too hard to mix with your fork, flour your hands and begin to pat it into a ball. Unless the recipe states otherwise, if the dough seems too wet, add a little more flour, and if it seems too dry, add a little more liquid.

If short on time, or if the dough is very sticky, use an electric stand mixer with a dough hook attachment.

kneading the dough

Kneading the dough is crucial to the bread-making process. It develops the gluten and causes the dough to become smooth and elastic as you work it. It also teaches you about the feel of the dough. Do not be tempted to add more and more flour as you knead, as this will produce a loaf that is tough and dry. You could use a smear of oil on the work surface instead of flour.

Take your ball of dough and roll it backwards and forwards, using your left hand to stretch it towards you and your right hand to push it away from you at the same time. Repeat this for 10 minutes until you have a smooth, springy, but soft dough that is quite elastic and no longer sticks to your hand. Work through the sticky phase until the dough develops a kind of smooth skin. To test if it is ready, you could try the stretch test: pull off a piece of dough and stretch it. It should be elastic enough not to break quickly when stretched out.

Bread dough can be mixed and kneaded, wrapped in cling film and frozen for up to 1 month. Let it thaw and come to room temperature before you remove the cling film, and prepare it for baking by either placing it in the prepared tins or on a baking sheet. Cover and leave to rise until doubled in size, and bake.

rising (proving) the dough

This is going to sound complicated, but isn't really. You should place the dough in a very sparingly oiled bowl, turning the dough around to coat it completely with a thin smearing of oil, to prevent a crust from forming on the surface of the dough. Cover the dough either with a kitchen towel or with cling film, and leave until the dough has just about doubled in size. The bowl should be big enough for the dough to rise without touching the cover, which would inhibit the rise. If you want the dough to rise quickly, put it somewhere warm, and if you want a fuller-flavoured loaf and have loads of time, leave it at room temperature or even overnight in the fridge. When it is ready, it will look puffed and soft. If touched with your finger, it should make an indentation that springs back out. If you over-prove the dough, crease marks will appear on the top of the dough, and it will begin to collapse. If this happens, you can re-form the dough and leave it to rise a second time; the yeast will continue to feed and the dough will swell again.

After rising once or twice, the dough usually needs to be punched down to deflate it. Transfer the dough to a lightly floured work surface and gently knead it again until all the air has been knocked out. Sometimes, all you need to do is roll the dough out to its required size. With very sticky dough recipes, you have to be careful not to knock the air out, but the recipe will explain the procedure.

baking the bread

Professional bakeries use steam in their ovens to create the perfect crispy crust. You can replicate this at home by placing a large roasting tin in the bottom of your oven to heat up, then adding enough hot water to fill it two-thirds full at the same time you put the bread into the oven to bake. Do not open the oven door for at least 5 minutes, but after that, you can check if the tin needs more water. You can also spray the top of the bread with water just before you place it in the oven.

For a softer crust, do not spray the dough and do not make any steam, and brush the crust with melted butter when you remove it from the oven.

For a golden, shiny crust, use an egg wash (egg beaten with a little water) just before baking. Do not get the egg wash on the loaf lin, as this will glue the bread into the tin and inhibit the rise.

For a soft, sweet crust, brush the dough with milk mixed with a little sugar just before baking.

For a sweet, sticky crust, brush the dough with sugar syrup or honey immediately after you remove it from the oven.

For a shiny, soft crust, brush the dough with olive oil just before and just after baking.

Bake the bread until the crust is golden brown. The bread should feel firm but not hard. If it is spongy, it is not cooked properly. If you tap the bottom of the loaf, it should have a hollow sound, and if it sounds dull, it needs more time in the oven.

Enriched dough is best baked at a low temperature to prevent the top from browning before the middle has cooked, and sweet bread generally burns more easily.

When baking rolls, spacing them further apart will make them crisper, and placing them close together, just touching, will produce softer rolls.

Cool your bread in the tin if required to do so in the recipe, and use wire racks to cool completely. Store bread in an airtight container for 1–3 days only.

troubleshooting

Here are a few problem-solving tips:
- If the loaf spread too much as it proved, the bread dough did not have enough flour in it.
- If the top crust separated from the rest of the loaf, there was too much flour in the dough, or it proved for too long.
- If the bread split while baking, it proved too long, or too much yeast was in the dough, or the loaf was formed with a large air pocket in the middle.
- If your bread collapsed during baking, the oven temperature was too low, or there was too much liquid or too much sugar, or you simply forgot the salt.
- If the dough did not rise much, too little yeast or too much salt was used. You may have used liquid that was too hot, or not enough liquid. Too much sugar interferes with the rise, and some flours do not contain enough gluten. You may have allowed the yeast and salt to interact with each other prior to mixing.
- This whole process may seem daunting at first, but it is an addictive and enjoyable hobby that can become obsessive as you explore the wonderful array of tantalising tastes and show your family and friends your skill and endeavours.

classic breads

In this chapter, you will find a number of classic

bread recipes that everyone knows about, and

from which other, more complicated loaves can

be developed.

basic white loaf

see variations page 38

The original and the best, this loaf has a light and fluffy centre with a crispy crust.

1 tsp sugar dissolved in 320 ml (11 fl oz) warm water
2 tsp active dry yeast
510 g (1 lb 2 oz) white bread flour

2 tsp salt
2 tbsp unsalted butter, softened
olive oil for greasing

Lightly grease a 900 g (2 lb) 23 x 13-cm (9 x 5-in) loaf tin with a little olive oil. Dissolve the sugar in the warm water and sprinkle the yeast on top. Set aside until frothy, about 10–15 minutes. In a large bowl, mix the flour and salt. Make a well in the centre and pour in the yeast liquid, add the butter and mix until a dough begins to form. Knead for about 10 minutes to make a smooth, soft and silky dough. Transfer to a large lightly oiled bowl and turn to coat it all over. Cover with cling film or a kitchen towel, and leave in a warm place for at least an hour, possibly 2 hours, until doubled in size.

Tip the dough on to a lightly floured work surface, knock back and knead a little more. Form the dough into an oblong shape the same width as the loaf tin, and roll up so that it is about 20–23 cm (8–9 in) long. Place it, seam underneath, in the loaf tin. Put the tin into a large lightly oiled plastic bag and leave to rise again in a warm place for about an hour, or until doubled in size, and springs back when you push your finger into it. Preheat the oven to 220°C (425°F) and place a roasting tin in the bottom of the oven to warm up. Remove the loaf tin from the plastic bag and dust the top with flour. Fill the roasting tin with hot water to create steam, place the bread in the oven and bake for 30 minutes, until the bottom of the loaf sounds hollow when tapped. Cool on a wire rack.

Makes 1 loaf

wholewheat honey bread

see variations page 39

Bread made with the wholegrain is better for your heart and keeps you fuller longer.

1 tsp sugar dissolved in 60 ml (2 fl oz) warm water
2 tsp active dry yeast
300 ml (10 fl oz) hot water
4 tbsp honey
2 tbsp white vegetable fat

255 g (9 oz) wholewheat flour, divided
320 g (11 oz) white bread flour, divided
1 tbsp wheatgerm
2 tsp salt
olive oil for greasing

Lightly grease a 900 g (2 lb) 23 x 13-cm (9 x 5-in) loaf tin with a little olive oil. Sprinkle the yeast on top of the sugar–water mix. Set aside for 10–15 minutes, until frothy. In a large bowl, mix the hot water with the honey and vegetable fat, and stir until they are melted. Set aside to cool until warm. Add the yeast liquid, half the wholewheat flour, 190 g (5$\frac{1}{2}$ oz) white bread flour, wheatgerm and salt, and mix well. Add the remaining wholewheat flour, and enough of the remaining white bread flour to make a slightly stiff dough. Turn the dough on to a lightly floured work surface, and knead for about 10 minutes to make a smooth and elastic dough. Shape into a ball, transfer to a large lightly oiled bowl and turn to coat it all over. Cover and leave in a warm place for about an hour, until doubled in size. Turn the dough out on to a lightly floured work surface, punch down and knead again. Form the dough into an oblong shape the same width as the tin, and roll up so that it is about 20–23 cm (8–9 in) long. Place it, seam underneath, in the loaf tin. Leave to rise again in a warm place for about an hour, or until doubled in size. Preheat the oven to 190°C (375°F). Remove the tin from the plastic bag, dust the top with flour and bake for 40–45 minutes, or until golden brown and the bottom of the loaf sounds hollow when tapped. Cool on a wire rack.

Makes 1 loaf

granary-style seeded malt bread

see variations page 40

This malted bread has a wonderfully unique flavour, which is developed with a little barley malt syrup and malted wheat flakes.

1 tsp + 1 tsp sugar, divided
415 ml (14 fl oz) warm water
2 tsp barley malt syrup or molasses
2 tsp active dry yeast
330 g (11¼ oz) white bread flour
280 g (10 oz) wholewheat flour
60 g (2 oz) malted wheat flakes

65 g (2¼ oz) rolled porridge oats
2 tbsp sunflower seeds
2 tbsp sesame seeds
2 tsp salt
2 tbsp olive oil + extra for greasing
a little beaten egg white for brushing
a few sunflower and pumpkin seeds for topping

Lightly grease a 900 g (2 lb) 23 x 13-cm (9 x 5-in) loaf tin with a little olive oil. Dissolve 1 teaspoon sugar in the warm water, add the barley malt syrup and stir to combine. Sprinkle the yeast on top and leave for 10–15 minutes until frothy.

In the bowl of a stand mixer with a dough hook attachment, mix together the white bread flour, wholewheat flour, malted wheat flakes, oats, seeds, salt and the remaining 1 teaspoon sugar. Make a well in the centre and pour in the yeast liquid. Add the olive oil and mix until a dough comes together. The dough should be soft and pliable, but not sticky. Knead on low speed for 5–8 minutes until the dough is smooth and elastic. Alternatively, mix in a large bowl, turn out on to a lightly floured work surface, and knead for about 10 minutes. Transfer to a large lightly oiled bowl and turn to coat it all over. Cover and leave in a warm place for 1 or 2 hours, until doubled in size.

Turn out on to a lightly floured work surface, punch down and form the dough into an oblong shape the same width as the tin. Roll up so that it is about 23 cm (8–9 in) long, the top is smooth and the seam is underneath. Place it, seam underneath, in the loaf tin. Put the tin into a large lightly oiled plastic bag and leave to rise again in a warm place for about an hour, or until the dough has doubled in size. Preheat the oven to 200°C (400°F). Remove the tin from the plastic bag, brush the top with a little beaten egg white, sprinkle with a few sunflower seeds and pumpkin seeds and bake for about 35 minutes, or until golden brown, well risen and sounds hollow when tapped underneath. Cool on a wire rack.

Makes 1 loaf

rustic country loaf

see variations page 41

This loaf is formed into an oval, not baked in a tin, and looks like the sort of bread you would find all across France.

1 tsp sugar dissolved in 320 ml (11 fl oz) warm water	510 g (1 lb 2 oz) white bread flour
2 tsp active dry yeast	1 tsp salt
	1 tbsp olive oil

Line a baking sheet with baking paper. Sprinkle the yeast on top of the sugar–water mix, and leave for 10–15 minutes until frothy. In a large bowl, mix the flour with the salt. Make a well in the centre, and add the yeast liquid and the olive oil. Mix well to form a soft dough. If it feels too dry, add more water, and if it feels too wet, add a little more flour. Knead for about 10 minutes, until the dough is soft, smooth and elastic. Transfer to a large lightly oiled bowl and turn to coat it all over. Cover and leave in a warm place for about an hour, until doubled in size.

Turn out on to a lightly floured surface, and punch down slightly. Mould into a round, slightly oval shape, and place on the lined baking sheet. Cover and leave for about an hour, until doubled in size.

Preheat the oven to 220°C (425°F). Dust the top of the loaf with flour, and make four deep diagonal slashes in the top of the loaf. Bake for about 30 minutes, or until the bottom of the loaf sounds hollow when tapped. Cool on a wire rack.

Makes 1 loaf

light rye

see variations page 42

This is a dark, satisfying loaf with a delicious chewy quality, slightly lightened with the addition of a little white flour. Makes great toast.

320 g (11 oz) rye flour
190 g (6¾ oz) white bread flour
1 tsp salt
1 tbsp instant dry yeast

355 ml (12 fl oz) warm water
1 tbsp molasses or honey
olive oil for greasing

Lightly grease a 900 g (2 lb) 23 x 13-cm (9 x 5-in) loaf tin with a little olive oil. In a large bowl, mix the flours together. Add the salt on one side and the yeast on the other. Mix the warm water and molasses or honey together, stirring until dissolved. Make a well in the centre of the flour, pour in the liquid and mix to form a sticky dough. If the dough feels too dry, add a little extra water, and if it feels too wet, add a little extra flour. Place the dough on a lightly floured work surface, and knead it with your hands and knuckles for about 5 minutes. It will feel less elastic than a normal white dough. Transfer to a large lightly oiled bowl and turn to coat it all over. Cover and leave in a warm place until doubled in size. It will take longer than white dough to rise, possibly as long as 3 hours.

Turn the dough out on to a lightly floured work surface, punch down and knead again briefly for a minute or two. Form into an oblong shape the same width as the tin, roll up and place in the tin with the seam underneath. Set aside for about 30 minutes while you preheat the oven to 220°C (425°F). Bake for 30 minutes. Remove from the oven, leave in the tin for 10 minutes and transfer to a wire rack to cool completely.

Makes 1 loaf

gluten-free seeded loaf

see variations page 43

This will look and feel quite different from a normal wheat loaf, but if you know someone who is wheat- or gluten-intolerant, this is a great bread to serve.

1 tsp sugar dissolved in 355 ml (12 fl oz) warm water
2 tsp dry yeast
175 g (6 oz) rice flour
90 g (3½ oz) tapioca flour
90 g (3½ oz) potato starch

2 tsp xanthan gum
1 tsp salt
3 eggs, room temperature
1 tbsp honey
1 tbsp olive oil + extra for greasing

1 tsp cider vinegar
1 tbsp poppy seeds
1 tbsp flaxseed (linseed)
1 tbsp sesame seeds
1 tsp of each of the above seeds for the topping

Lightly grease a 450 g (1 lb) 20 x 10-cm (8 x 4-in) loaf tin with a little oil. Sprinkle the yeast on top of the sugar–water mix, and leave for 10–15 minutes until frothy. In a large bowl, combine the rice flour, tapioca flour and potato starch, and stir in the xanthan gum and salt. In another bowl, whisk the eggs, honey, oil and vinegar until frothy. Make a well in the centre of the flour and pour in the yeast liquid, the egg liquid, and the seeds. Mix with an electric mixer for 4 minutes. Scoop into the loaf tin, cover loosely with lightly oiled cling film and let the dough rise until it is 2.5 cm (1 in) above the top of the tin.

Preheat the oven to 190°C (375°F). Sprinkle the top of the loaf with extra seeds and bake for 50–60 minutes. Remove from the oven and leave to cool in the tin for 10 minutes, then turn out and leave to cool completely on a wire rack before slicing.

Makes 1 loaf

irish soda bread

see variations page 44

There is no yeast in this bread; the rise comes from bicarbonate of soda. It's so quick to make, you can throw it together in just a few minutes – but be sure to eat it the same day, as it does not keep well.

475 g (1 lb 1 oz) plain flour
1 tsp bicarbonate of soda

1 tsp salt
395 ml (13 fl oz) buttermilk

Preheat the oven to 220°C (425°F) and line a large baking sheet with baking paper. In a large bowl, mix the flour, bicarbonate of soda and salt together. Make a well in the centre and add the buttermilk. Mix quickly to form a sticky dough. Turn it out on to a lightly floured work surface and form quickly into a ball. Place it on the baking sheet, flatten the ball slightly with your hand and cut a deep cross in the top. Dust with a little flour and bake for 30 minutes, or until the bottom of the loaf sounds hollow when tapped. Cool on a wire rack.

Makes 1 loaf

focaccia

see variations page 45

Slightly more challenging to make than regular white bread, as the dough is wetter, this Italian bread is wonderful dipped in an herb-and-garlic-infused olive oil (see variations).

510 g (1 lb 2 oz) white bread flour
1 tsp salt
1¹/₂ tsp active dry yeast
355 ml (12 fl oz) warm water, divided

3 tbsp extra virgin olive oil + extra for greasing
  and drizzling
coarse sea salt for sprinkling
2 rosemary sprigs, separated into small pieces

Line 2 large baking sheets with baking paper, and lightly grease a 28 x 23-cm (11 x 9-in) rectangular glass baking dish with a little olive oil. Mix the flour and salt together in a large bowl. In a small bowl, mix the yeast with 300 ml (10 fl oz) warm water and stir to dissolve the yeast. Set aside for 5 minutes. Make a well in the centre of the flour and add the yeast liquid and 3 tablespoons olive oil. Turn the mixture around with either a plastic dough scraper or your hands. Gradually add the rest of the water until a sticky dough is formed. You may not have to use all of it. Turn the dough out on to a lightly floured or oiled work surface. Using either your hands and knuckles, or a plastic dough scraper, knead the dough for about 10 minutes, until it is smooth and elastic. The dough will be wetter at first, but will form a smooth skin. Transfer to the oiled dish, cover with a kitchen towel and leave in a warm place to rise, about an hour.

Lightly flour the work surface, and carefully tip the dough out on to it. Try not to knock the air out. Cut the dough in half and stretch each half into a rectangle. Carefully lift on to the baking sheets, place each one in a greased plastic bag and leave for about an hour, until doubled in size.

Preheat the oven to 220°C (425°F). Remove the baking sheets from the plastic bags and make deep dimples in the dough with your fingers. Drizzle each focaccia with 1–2 tablespoons olive oil and sprinkle with coarse sea salt. Push small rosemary sprigs into the dough. Bake for 15 minutes, or until the tops are golden brown and the bottom of the loaves sound hollow when tapped.

Makes 2 loaves

quick & easy ciabatta

see variations page 46

An authentic ciabatta can be complicated and tricky to make, so this is a simplified but delicious recipe that is ideal for beginners.

510 g (1 lb 2 oz) white bread flour
$\frac{1}{2}$ tsp sugar
1$\frac{1}{2}$ tsp active dry yeast

440 ml (15 fl oz) + 2 tbsp warm water, divided
1 tsp salt
1 tbsp extra virgin olive oil

Line a large baking sheet with baking paper. In a large bowl, mix the flour with the sugar and yeast, add the warm water and salt and stir them round with your hands. Raise bits of the dough up high and slap them down again to aerate the mixture. This develops the dough's characteristic airy texture. Alternatively, knead in a food mixer with a dough hook, but finish the process with your hands. Pour the olive oil over the dough, cover the bowl with cling film and leave in a warm place for about an hour, until doubled in size.

Preheat the oven to 200°C (400°F). Carefully pour the dough on to a well-floured work surface and, without knocking the air out, fold the dough over lengthways like an envelope to create the flat ciabatta loaf. Transfer the dough on to the baking sheet and bake for 30–40 minutes, or until the bread is golden and sounds hollow when tapped on the bottom.

Makes 1 loaf

multi-grain bread

see variations page 47

The different grains add interest and texture to make a tasty loaf with plenty of fibre.

1 tsp sugar dissolved in 240 ml (8 fl oz) warm
water and 120 ml (4 fl oz) warm whole milk
4 tbsp honey
2 tsp active dry yeast
250 g (9 oz) white bread flour

320 g (11 oz) wholewheat flour
1 tsp salt
2 tbsp wheatgerm
2 tbsp oat bran
4 tbsp olive oil + extra for greasing

Lightly grease a 900 g (2 lb) 23 x 13-cm (9 x 5-in) loaf tin with a little olive oil. Stir the honey into the sugar–water–milk mix, and sprinkle the yeast on top. Leave for 10–15 minutes until frothy. In a large bowl, mix the white and wholewheat flours with the salt, wheatgerm and oat bran. Make a well in the centre and add the yeast liquid and the olive oil. Mix well to form a soft dough. Knead for about 10 minutes, until the dough is soft, smooth and elastic.

Transfer the dough to a large lightly oiled bowl, and turn to coat it all over. Cover and put in a warm place for about an hour, until doubled in size. Turn out on to a lightly floured work surface, punch down and knead a little more. Form the dough into an oblong shape the same width as the tin, and roll up so that it is about 20–23 cm (8–9 in) long. Place it, seam underneath, in the loaf tin. Leave to rise again in a warm place for about an hour, or until doubled in size. Preheat the oven to 200°C (400°F). When the dough is ready, bake for 30 minutes or until the bottom of the loaf sounds hollow when tapped.

Makes 1 loaf

sourdough

see variations page 48

Sourdough takes a lot of patience, but the end result is definitely worth it!

sourdough starter
285 g (10 oz) white bread flour + extra for
   feeding
300 ml (10 fl oz) water + extra for feeding

to complete the sourdough loaf
600 g (1 lb 5¼ oz) white bread flour
1 or 2 tsp salt
extra flour and polenta

To form the starter, mix the flour with the water in a medium bowl to form a thick paste. Transfer to a glass or plastic (avoid metal) container with the lid left slightly ajar and leave at room temperature for 3–4 days. After this time it should be bubbling and have a sour smell. Discard half the mixture. Mix 120 g (4 oz) flour and 170 ml (6 fl oz) water into a paste and add it to the original mixture. This is called feeding the starter. Transfer the starter to a large plastic container with a tightly fitting lid, and the following day it will be ready to use to make sourdough bread. You will usually need half the quantity to make a recipe. Store the remainder in the fridge and take it out the night before you need to use it each time. Each time you use half, feed it again, and return it to the fridge. Do not use when it has only just been fed. If it fails to bubble, throw it out and start again.

In a large bowl, mix 600 g (1 lb 5¼ oz) flour with 250 g (8 oz) starter and enough water to make a soft but manageable dough. Set aside for about 15 minutes, and knead in the salt. Transfer it to a lightly oiled bowl, cover and leave at a room temperature of 22–24°C (71–75°F) until doubled in size. This could take about 5 hours. Prepare a large colander lined with a clean kitchen towel. Dust with polenta or flour to prevent sticking. Tip the risen dough on to a lightly floured work surface, and fold inwards repeatedly until the dough is smooth

and all the air has been knocked out. Form into a ball, place it in the colander and dust with more polenta or flour. Cover with a clean towel and set aside at room temperature until doubled in size, about 12–14 hours. If it is wrinkly when you return to it, it has over-proved. Reshape it without kneading it again, and leave to prove once more, although this should take half the time. When the dough is ready, preheat the oven to 200°C (400°F) and line a large baking sheet with baking paper. Tip the dough upside down on to the baking sheet and cut a deep slash in what is now the top. Bake for 30–40 minutes, or until the top is golden brown and the bottom of the loaf sounds hollow when tapped.

Makes 1 loaf

italian crusty loaf

see variations page 49

This has a delicious crispy crust and a soft, light and fluffy centre. This loaf freezes well.

1 tbsp fine polenta	365 g (13 oz) white bread flour	1 tsp salt
250 ml (8 fl oz) warm water	½ tbsp sugar	1 egg white, lightly beaten
2 tsp active dry yeast	1 tbsp extra virgin olive oil	1 tbsp poppy seeds

Generously dust a large baking sheet with fine polenta. Place the warm water and the yeast in a large bowl and leave for 5 minutes, until frothy. Add the flour and sugar to the water and mix until a dough starts to form. Drizzle the oil and salt into the dough and mix for 8–10 minutes, or until a smooth, firm and elastic dough is formed. Transfer the dough to a lightly oiled bowl, and turn to coat it all over. Cover and put in a warm place for about 1½ hours, until doubled in size. Turn the dough out on to a lightly oiled work surface, punch down to remove most of the air and press into a large rectangle. Roll it up tightly, sealing the seam well. Repeat pressing, rolling and sealing 3 or 4 times. The dough should finish as an oval shape, with tapered ends. Place the dough on to the baking sheet. Cover and put in a warm place for about 1½ hours, until doubled in size. Preheat the oven to 220°C (425°F), and place a roasting tin in the bottom and half fill it with hot water. Brush the loaves all over with the beaten egg white and sprinkle the poppy seeds over the top. With a sharp knife, score three or four 6 mm (¼ in)-deep slashes diagonally across the top of each one. Spray the loaves generously with water and place in the oven. After 3 minutes, open the oven door and spray the loaves again with water. Turn the oven temperature down to 180°C (350°F) and bake the bread for another 25–35 minutes, or until golden brown and the bottom of the loaves sound hollow when tapped. Cool on a wire rack.

Makes 2 loaves

variations

basic white loaf

see base recipe page 17

australian fairy bread
Prepare the basic recipe. When cold, slice the bread, spread each slice with a thin layer of butter and sprinkle with hundreds and thousands. Cut into four slices diagonally.

cottage loaf
Prepare the basic recipe. Separate the dough into two thirds and one third, shape both pieces into balls, cover and leave for 5 minutes. Put the smaller one on top of the larger one, and push a floured wooden spoon handle through the centre of both rounds to join them together. With a sharp knife, slash cuts around the edge of both rounds. Prove for a second time and bake as directed.

feta cheese & shallot loaf
Prepare the basic recipe, sprinkling 100 g (3½ oz) diced feta cheese and 1 small finely chopped shallot on to the oblong of dough just before rolling it up to go in the tin.

basil tomato parmesan bread
Prepare the basic recipe, adding 2 tablespoons finely grated Parmesan cheese and 2 teaspoons dried basil to the flour and salt. Sprinkle a few chopped sundried tomatoes on to the oblong of dough just before rolling it up to go in the tin.

variations

wholewheat honey bread

see base recipe page 19

coconut bran bread
Prepare the basic recipe, using wheatbran in place of wheatgerm, and adding 25 g (1 oz) flaked coconut to the flour mix.

sunflower seed bread
Prepare the basic recipe, adding 3 tablespoons raw shelled sunflower seeds to the flour mix.

brown sugar pecan bread
Prepare the basic recipe, omitting the honey and substituting 75 g (2½ oz) brown sugar, added to the flour mix with 40 g (1½ oz) chopped pecans.

orange cumin bread
Prepare the basic recipe, adding 1 tablespoon grated orange zest and ¾ teaspoon ground cumin to the flour mix.

granary-style seeded malt bread

see base recipe page 20

mango macadamia nut bread
Prepare the basic recipe, omitting the barley malt syrup and the sunflower and sesame seeds. Substitute 30 g (1 oz) chopped macadamia nuts and 30 g (1 oz) mango purée, added with the olive oil.

ginger apple sauce bread
Prepare the basic recipe, omitting the barley malt syrup and the sunflower and sesame seeds. Substitute 30 g (1 oz) apple sauce and 1 teaspoon ground ginger, added with the olive oil.

oatmeal walnut bread
Prepare the basic recipe. Use honey and 30 g (1 oz) chopped walnuts in place of the barley malt syrup and the sunflower and sesame seeds.

granary-style rolls
Prepare the basic recipe. Turn the dough out on to a lightly floured work surface, divide into 24 equal portions and roll into balls. Place on lined baking sheets, cover and leave for 30–40 minutes. Bake in a preheated oven at 230°C (450°F) for 15–20 minutes.

variations

rustic country loaf

see base recipe page 23

fig & cracked black pepper country loaf
Prepare the basic recipe, adding 340 g (12 oz) roughly chopped dried ready-to-eat figs and
2 teaspoons cracked black pepper with the olive oil.

chocolate french toast
Prepare the basic recipe and cut into about 10 slices. Dissolve 130 g (1 oz) unsweetened
cocoa powder in 60 ml (2 fl oz) hot water; allow to cool. Whisk together 4 eggs, 180 ml
(6 fl oz) double cream, 180 ml (6 fl oz) milk, 60 g (2 oz) sugar, 1 teaspoon vanilla extract and
½ teaspoon salt. Add cocoa mix. Dip two slices of bread at a time in the chocolate batter,
and fry in hot butter for 3 minutes each side. Dust with icing sugar and serve with syrup.

tomato & pepper bruschetta
Prepare the basic recipe and cut into about 10 slices. Grill on both sides. Rub half a garlic
clove over each slice. Mix together 4–5 roasted red peppers, 2 crushed garlic cloves, 15 g
(½ oz) torn basil leaves and 30 g (1 oz) chopped sundried tomatoes. Spread the mix on
the slices.

green olive country loaf
Prepare the basic recipe, adding 340 g (12 oz) chopped pitted green olives to the flour with
the yeast liquid.

variations

light rye

see base recipe page 24

onion & dill rye
Prepare the basic recipe, adding 1 tablespoon dried onion and 2 teaspoons dried dill to the flour.

prune & walnut rye
Prepare the basic recipe, using 60 g (2 oz) bran flakes in place of 60 g (2 oz) rye flour. Add 75 g (3 oz) chopped pitted prunes and 3 tablespoons chopped walnuts to the flour.

salt beef on rye
Prepare the basic recipe, cut into nine slices and cut each one into two triangles. Mix 2 tablespoons Dijon mustard with 2 tablespoons mayonnaise and spread a little on each triangle. Cut 125 g (4 oz) salt beef into 18 pieces, add to the triangles and top with a slice or two of pickled cucumber.

caraway light rye
Prepare the basic recipe, adding 1 teaspoon caraway seeds to the bowl with the flours.

variations

gluten-free seeded loaf

see base recipe page 26

gluten-free parmesan & chive seeded loaf
Prepare the basic recipe, adding 2 tablespoons grated Parmesan cheese and 2 teaspoons dried chives to the bowl with the yeast liquid.

gluten-free chilli & coriander sandwich loaf
Prepare the basic recipe, omitting the seeds. Substitute 1 seeded and finely chopped red chilli and 2 tablespoons freshly chopped coriander, and sprinkle the top of the loaf with 2 teaspoons crushed red pepper flakes.

gluten-free garlic & thyme sandwich loaf
Prepare the basic recipe, omitting the seeds. Substitute 1 teaspoon garlic powder and 1 teaspoon dried thyme.

gluten-free sundried tomato & basil seeded loaf
Prepare the basic recipe, adding 30 g (1 oz) finely chopped sundried tomatoes and 15 g (1/2 oz) finely chopped basil leaves to the bowl with the yeast liquid.

variations

irish soda bread

see base recipe page 27

sundried tomato soda bread rolls
Prepare the basic recipe, adding 30 g (1 oz) finely chopped sundried tomatoes and 1 teaspoon thyme to the flour mix. Handling as little as possible, cut the dough into five equal portions and form into balls. Flatten, place on a lined baking sheet, mark a cross in the top and bake in a preheated oven at 200°C (400°F) for 20–25 minutes.

dill & poppy seed soda bread
Prepare the basic recipe, adding 1 teaspoon dried dill and 1 tablespoon poppy seeds to the flour mix.

cheese & mustard soda bread
Prepare the basic recipe, adding 30 g (1 oz) grated cheddar cheese and 2 teaspoons dry mustard to the flour mix.

spicy mexican soda bread
Prepare the basic recipe, adding 4 finely chopped green onions, 1 seeded, finely chopped red chilli and 30 g (1 oz) finely grated cheddar cheese to the flour mix.

variations

focaccia

see base recipe page 28

garlic, courgette & basil focaccia
Prepare the basic recipe, omitting the rosemary. Instead, scatter 2 small, finely sliced courgettes and 2 teaspoons dried basil over the focaccias.

red onion & thyme focaccia
Prepare the basic recipe, omitting the rosemary. Instead, scatter 2 finely sliced red onions and 2 teaspoons dried thyme over the focaccias.

mozzarella & pesto focaccia
Prepare the basic recipe, omitting the rosemary. Instead, push small pieces of mozzarella into the surface of the focaccia and drizzle with pesto.

black olive & goat cheese focaccia
Prepare the basic recipe, omitting the rosemary. Instead, push small pieces of goat's cheese into the surface of the focaccia and scatter with chopped pitted black olives.

variations

quick & easy ciabatta

see base recipe page 31

garlic ciabatta
Prepare the basic recipe, adding 2 crushed garlic cloves to the flour in the bowl.

black pepper & flaked sea salt ciabatta
Prepare the basic recipe, adding 2 tablespoons freshly ground black pepper to the flour.
While still hot, brush with melted butter and sprinkle with flaked sea salt.

ciabatta rolls
Prepare the basic recipe. After folding the dough like an envelope, very carefully cut the
dough into eight or nine rectangles with a sharp knife. Try not to knock out the air. Place on
the baking sheet and proceed as directed.

chilli ciabatta
Prepare the basic recipe, adding 2 teaspoons crushed red pepper flakes to the bowl with
the flour.

variations

multi-grain bread

see base recipe page 32

multi-grain bread with walnuts
Prepare the basic recipe, adding 40 g (1½ oz) chopped walnuts to the bowl with the flour.

multi-grain bread with rosemary & thyme
Prepare the basic recipe, adding 2 teaspoons dried rosemary and 2 teaspoons dried thyme to the bowl with the flour.

multi-grain seedy bread
Prepare the basic recipe, adding 2 tablespoons each of sunflower seeds, sesame seeds, onion seeds and poppy seeds to the bowl with the flour.

multi-grain blue cheese & pecan bread
Prepare the basic recipe, adding 40 g (1½ oz) chopped pecans to the bowl with the flour. Crumble 175 g (6 oz) blue cheese over the dough just before rolling up to go in the tin. Proceed as directed.

variations

sourdough

see base recipe page 34

lemon & rosemary sourdough
Prepare the basic recipe. Add 1 tablespoon grated lemon zest and 2 teaspoons dried rosemary to the bowl with the flour and starter. Proceed as directed.

cheese & bacon sourdough
Prepare the basic recipe. Add 4 slices of bacon that have been cooked until crispy and crumbled, and 3 tablespoons grated Parmesan cheese to the bowl with the flour and starter.

seedy sourdough
Prepare the basic recipe. Add 2 tablespoons each of sunflower seeds, sesame seeds, onion seeds and poppy seeds to the bowl with the flour and starter. Proceed as directed.

chocolate chip & almond sourdough
Prepare the basic recipe. Add 60 g (2 oz) dark chocolate chips and 3 tablespoons chopped almonds to the bowl with the flour and starter.

variations

italian crusty loaf

see base recipe page 37

lemon & poppy seed crusty loaf
Prepare the basic recipe, adding 2 teaspoons grated lemon zest and 1 tablespoon poppy seeds to the flour.

cardamom & thyme loaf
Prepare the basic recipe, adding 1 teaspoon crushed cardamom seeds and 2 teaspoons dried thyme to the flour.

chilli & parmesan crusty loaf
Prepare the basic recipe, adding 2 teaspoons crushed red chilli flakes and 20 g ($^2/_3$ oz) grated Parmesan cheese to the flour.

italian crusty loaf with pesto swirl
Prepare the basic recipe. After first rising, roll the dough out to two 20 x 35-cm (8 x 14-in) rectangles and spread 4 tablespoons pesto over each one. Roll them up like Swiss rolls and place them on the baking sheets with the seams underneath. Proceed as directed.

breakfast breads

In this chapter, you will find exciting ways to start your day, from banana pecan loaf to orange and cinnamon swirl bread to Danish pastries.

maple pecan breakfast bread

see variations page 67

This delicious and succulent loaf is full of tasty pecans and moist bananas, and sweetened with maple syrup.

255 g (9 oz) plain flour
170 g (6 oz) sugar
³/₄ tsp bicarbonate of soda
¹/₂ tsp salt
150 g (6 oz) toasted, coarsely chopped pecans
4 very ripe bananas
60 ml (2 fl oz) natural yoghurt

2 eggs, lightly beaten
6 tbsp butter, melted and cooled + extra for
    greasing
1¹/₂ tsp vanilla extract
10 pecan halves for the topping
85 g (3 oz) maple syrup

Preheat the oven to 180°C (350°F) and grease a 450 g (1 lb) 20 x 10-cm (8 x 4-in) loaf tin with a little butter. In a large bowl, stir together the flour, sugar, bicarbonate of soda, salt and chopped pecans until well mixed. In a medium bowl, mash 3 of the bananas and chop 1. Add the yoghurt, beaten eggs, melted and cooled butter and vanilla extract, and stir together with a wooden spoon. Tip the wet ingredients into the dry ingredients, and fold together lightly and gently until just combined. Transfer to the loaf tin and decorate the top with the pecan halves. Drizzle the maple syrup over the top of the loaf. Bake for 45–55 minutes, until golden brown and cooked through, and a cocktail stick inserted into the centre comes out clean. Leave to cool in the tin for 5 minutes, then transfer to a wire rack to cool. Serve warm.

Makes 1 loaf

hot cinnamon ring

see variations page 68

Buttermilk biscuits layered in a fluted tin with butter and maple syrup mixed with brown sugar and pecans – what's not to like?

for the biscuits
255 g (9 oz) plain flour
$^1/_4$ tsp bicarbonate of soda
1 tbsp baking powder
1 tsp salt
6 tbsp unsalted butter, chilled + extra for
    greasing
240 ml (8 fl oz) buttermilk

to finish
3 tbsp butter
170 g (6 oz) maple syrup
60 g (2 oz) brown sugar
1 tsp cinnamon
40 g (1$^1/_2$ oz) chopped pecans
40 g (1$^1/_2$ oz) sliced almonds

Grease a 25 x 8-cm (10 x 3$^1/_2$-in) fluted tin. Place the flour, bicarbonate of soda, baking powder and salt into the bowl of a food processor. Cut the butter into small pieces and add to the flour. Pulse until the mixture looks like fine breadcrumbs. Add the buttermilk and pulse a few times until just combined. If the dough fails to come together, add a little more buttermilk and pulse again. Turn out on to a lightly floured work surface and gently press the dough out until it is about 1.5 cm ($^1/_2$ in) thick. Do not roll, as this will make the biscuits tough; the dough should be handled as little and as lightly as possible. Fold the dough four or five times, and gently press into a round, 2.5 cm (1 in) thick. With a 5-cm (2-in) plain or fluted cutter, press out about 10 biscuits, place them on the baking sheet and chill until required.

Preheat the oven to 190°C (375°F). In a small pan over a gentle heat, melt the butter and syrup together, and set aside to cool slightly. In a small bowl, mix the brown sugar with the

cinnamon and nuts. Pour half the melted butter and syrup into the bottom of the fluted tin, and sprinkle half the brown sugar and nut mixture around the tin. Place the uncooked biscuits around the tin, overlapping them closely. Pour the remaining syrup over the biscuits and sprinkle the rest of the sugar and nuts on top. Bake for 25–30 minutes, or until golden brown on top and cooked through. Leave to cool in the tin for 2 minutes, then invert on to a serving plate. Serve warm.

Makes 8 servings

fruity malt loaf

see variations page 69

This is delicious sliced and spread liberally with butter and honey.

1 tsp sugar
190 ml (6½ fl oz) + 1 tbsp warm water
2 tsp active dry yeast
450 g (1 lb) plain flour
1 tsp salt

85 g (3 oz) sultanas
3 tbsp barley malt syrup
2 tbsp molasses or black treacle
2 tbsp butter + extra for greasing
2 tbsp honey for glazing

Grease two 450 g (1 lb) 20 x 10-cm (8 x 4-in) loaf tins with a little butter. In a medium bowl, dissolve the sugar in the warm water, add the yeast and leave until frothy, about 10–15 minutes. In a large bowl, sieve together the flour and salt. Add the sultanas. Set aside. In a small pan over a gentle heat, warm together the barley malt syrup, molasses and butter. Cool slightly and add to the flour mixture, mixing well until a dough comes together. If the dough feels too dry, add a little more water, and if it feels too wet, add extra flour. Turn out on to a lightly floured work surface and knead for 8–10 minutes until soft, smooth and elastic.

Divide the dough in half, flatten each piece to the same width as the tins and roll up as for a Swiss roll. Drop into the tins, place the tins inside lightly oiled plastic bags and put in a warm place for 45 minutes, or until the dough rises to the top of the tins and springs back when lightly pressed. Preheat the oven to 200°C (400°F). Remove the bags and bake the loaves for 40–45 minutes, until the bottom of the loaves sound hollow when tapped. Turn the loaves out of the tins on to a wire rack, and brush the top of the hot loaves with a wet brush dipped in honey. Allow to cool.

Makes 2 loaves

jam doughnuts

see variations page 70

Such a traditional breakfast treat cannot be beaten for simplicity and taste.

320 g (11 oz) white bread flour
60 g (2 oz) sugar
4 tsp active dry yeast
1 tsp salt
9 tbsp warm whole milk
6 tbsp warm water

60 g (2 oz) unsalted butter, room temperature
2 eggs, room temperature, lightly beaten
4–5 tbsp strawberry or raspberry jam
75 g (3 oz) sugar mixed with 1 tsp cinnamon
    for coating
about 2 litres (4 pints) sunflower oil for frying

In the large bowl of a stand mixer, combine the flour and sugar. Add the yeast on one side and the salt on the other. In a medium bowl, mix the warm milk, warm water and butter, and stir until the butter has just melted. Make a well in the centre of the flour mixture, and add the milk mixture and eggs. With a dough hook attachment, mix until the dough comes together. Knead for about 5–8 minutes, until smooth and elastic. Transfer to a large lightly oiled bowl, and turn the dough around to coat it all over. Cover and put in a warm place for an hour or so, until doubled in size. Shape into 12 balls, folding the edges of the balls underneath until smooth, turning as you go. Place the doughnuts on a lightly floured baking sheet, spacing them well apart. Leave to rise again for 45 minutes. Make a hole in the side of each round with the handle of a wooden spoon, and fill with ½ teaspoon of jam. Pinch the dough back into shape, enclosing the jam inside. In a very large pan, heat enough oil to come two thirds up the side of the pan. When it has reached 157°C (315°F), fry the doughnuts in batches for about 3 minutes each side, flipping them over carefully. Blot with paper towels and roll in sugar and cinnamon until coated all over. Serve warm.

Makes 12 doughnuts

orange & cinnamon swirl bread

see variations page 71

This bread is so pretty when you cut into it, showing the delicious swirl of cinnamon, brown sugar and apricot jam.

1 tsp + 3 tbsp sugar, divided
160 ml (5 fl oz) warm water
2 tsp active dry yeast
450 g (1 lb) plain flour
2 tsp salt
2 eggs, beaten

juice and finely grated zest of 1 orange
5 tbsp apricot jam
1 tbsp cinnamon
85 g (3 oz) brown sugar
oil for greasing

Grease two 450 g (1 lb) 20 x 10-cm (8 x 4-in) loaf tins with a little oil. Dissolve 1 teaspoon sugar in the warm water, sprinkle the yeast on top and leave for 10–15 minutes until frothy. In a large bowl, mix together the flour, salt and 3 tablespoons sugar. Add the yeast liquid, eggs, juice and zest of orange, and work to a firm dough. Turn out on to a lightly floured work surface and knead for 10 minutes, until the dough is smooth and elastic. Place the dough in a large lightly oiled bowl, and turn so that it is coated all over. Cover and put in a warm place for about 1¹/₂ hours, until doubled in size. Turn the dough out on to a lightly floured work surface and punch down. Knead for a few minutes until the dough is firm. Roll into two 15 x 33-cm (6 x 13-in) rectangles. Spread each one with apricot jam, and sprinkle with cinnamon and brown sugar. Roll up each rectangle like a Swiss roll and place in the loaf tins. Put in a warm place for about 30 minutes, until doubled in size. Preheat the oven to 200°C (400°F). Bake the loaves for 30–35 minutes, until the top is golden brown and the bottom of the loaves make a hollow sound when tapped. Cool on a wire rack.

Makes 2 loaves

chocolate–pistachio espresso bread

see variations page 72

This is a very chocolaty quick bread with a kick of coffee to get you going in the morning, and garnished with pistachios for a bit of crunch.

190 g (6½ oz) plain flour
45 g (1½ oz) unsweetened cocoa powder
2 tsp baking powder
½ tsp salt
1 tbsp instant coffee powder
2 eggs, room temperature
200 g (7 oz) sugar

125 ml (4½ fl. oz) canola oil
250 g (9 oz) Greek yoghurt
1 tsp vanilla extract
115 g (4 oz) + 4 tbsp. shelled chopped pistachio nuts, divided
butter for greasing

Preheat oven to 180°C (350°F) and grease a 450 g (1 lb) 20 x 10-cm (8 x 4-in) loaf pan with a little butter. Dust the pan lightly with flour. In a small bowl, sieve together the flour, cocoa powder, baking powder and salt. Stir in the coffee powder and set aside. In a large mixing bowl, With an electric mixer on medium speed, beat the eggs and sugar until smooth. Add oil, yoghurt and vanilla extract, and beat until well combined. Stir in the flour mixture and half of the pistachio nuts. Pour the batter into the pan, smooth the top, and sprinkle on the remaining pistachio nuts. Bake for 45–50 minutes, until the top is dry and a toothpick inserted into the centre comes out clean. Cool in the pan for 10 minutes, then turn out onto a wire rack to cool completely. Serve warm or cold.

Makes 1 loaf

light & flaky croissants

see variations page 73

This is a simplified version of croissants, but still takes quite a bit of time. Start the day before, refrigerate overnight, bring back to room temperature and leave for an hour or so to rise until doubled in size before baking.

60 g (2 oz) + 1 tsp sugar, divided
240 ml (8 fl oz) warm milk
2 tsp active dry yeast
510 g (1 lb 2 oz) white bread flour
1 egg, room temperature,
    lightly beaten

100 g (4 oz) softened (not
    melted) + 200 g (8 oz)
    very cold butter, divided
1 tsp salt

for the glaze
1 tsp sugar
2 tsp water
1 egg, room temperature,
    lightly beaten

Dissolve the sugar in the warm milk, sprinkle the yeast on top and leave for 10–15 minutes until frothy. Add 100 g (3^1/$_2$ oz) flour and beat well. Add remaining 1 teaspoon sugar and egg, and beat again until smooth. Add the softened butter, beat and set aside. Put the rest of the flour and salt into the bowl of a food processor. Add the cold butter, cut into small cubes, and pulse briefly until butter is the size of peas. The idea now is to get a soft dough without melting the pieces of butter, so it needs to stay really cold. Tip the flour and butter mixture into a large bowl, add the milk and yeast mixture, and mix until moistened. Cover the bowl and refrigerate for 2 hours. Remove the bowl from the fridge, turn out on to a lightly floured surface and knead lightly. Roll the dough into a rectangle about 45 x 30 cm (18 x 12 in). Working as quickly as possible, fold the dough into thirds, bringing the bottom third up and folding the top third down. Put into a greased plastic bag and back into the fridge for 1 hour. Repeat the rolling and chilling twice more. You can leave the dough in the fridge overnight at this stage.

Divide the dough into four parts. Keep three parts chilled, and roll out the fourth into a rectangle the same size as before. Cut into two strips and cut each strip into six triangles. Hold down the wide base of the triangle, pull the other end slightly to cause a slight tension in the dough, and then roll up into a croissant. Either leave straight or curve ends in for a more traditional look. Place on floured baking sheets and cover loosely. Repeat with remaining dough. Let croissants rise at room temperature until doubled in size. This could take 2 hours. Preheat the oven to 200°C (400°F). For the glaze, make an egg wash by mixing the sugar and water, then adding the egg. Remove cover from croissants, brush with egg wash and place in the oven. Immediately turn temperature down to 180°C (350°F) and bake for 15–20 minutes, until golden brown and cooked through. Serve warm.

Makes 24 croissants

brioche

see variations page 74

You will need twelve 7-cm (3-in) brioche tins for these sweet little buns.

250 g (9 oz) white bread flour
½ tsp salt
1 tbsp sugar
3 tbsp warm water
2 tsp active dry yeast

2 eggs, room temperature, lightly beaten,
   plus extra for brushing
2 tbsp butter, melted
oil for brushing

In a large bowl, sieve the flour and salt together. Dissolve the sugar in the warm water, sprinkle the yeast on top and put in a warm place for 10–15 minutes, until frothy. Make a well in the centre of the flour, and add the yeast liquid, eggs and melted butter. With a wooden spoon, beat the dough until it leaves the sides of the bowl clean, turn it out on to a lightly floured surface and knead for 5 minutes. Put the dough into a large oiled bowl and turn it around to coat all over. Cover and leave at room temperature for an hour or more, until doubled in size. Turn the dough out on to a lightly floured work surface and knead again, until smooth. Shape dough into a long sausage and cut into 12 equal pieces. Brush the brioche tins with oil, and shape three-quarters of each piece into a ball. Place them in the tins. With a floured finger, press a hole into the centre of each bun as far as the base of the tin. Shape the remaining pieces of dough into balls and insert them into the holes. Press lightly to join the two pieces of dough. When all 12 brioche have been shaped, set the tins on a baking sheet, cover loosely and rise until the dough is just below the tops of the tins. Preheat the oven to 230°C (450°F). Remove the cover, brush the tops of the brioche with beaten egg and bake for 10 minutes or until golden brown. Turn out and cool on a wire rack.

Makes 12 brioche

chocolate & peanut butter bread

see variations page 75

Sliced, toasted and buttered for breakfast, this pretty loaf is a perfect weekend treat.

320 g (11 oz) plain flour
1 tsp baking powder
1 tsp bicarbonate of soda
½ tsp salt
60 g (2 oz) dark chocolate
   chips
60 g (2 oz) peanut butter
   chips

2 medium bananas, mashed
180 g (6¼ oz) creamy peanut
   butter
100 g (4 oz) sugar
85 g (3 oz) brown sugar
2 eggs, room temperature
1 tsp vanilla extract
120 ml (4 fl oz) whole milk

30 g (1 oz) unsweetened
   cocoa powder
butter for greasing

for the topping
2 tbsp dark chocolate chips
2 tbsp peanut butter chips

Preheat oven to 180°C (350°F) and grease a 450 g (1 lb) 20 x 10-cm (8 x 4-in) loaf tin with a little butter. Dust the tin lightly with flour. In a medium bowl, sieve together the flour, baking powder, bicarbonate of soda and salt. Stir in the chocolate chips and peanut butter chips. In a large mixing bowl, with a mixer on medium speed, beat together the banana and peanut butter until creamy, add the sugar and brown sugar, and beat for another minute. Beat in the eggs, one at a time, and the vanilla, until smooth. On slow speed, gradually add the flour mixture and milk, alternating between the two, until well combined. Transfer half of the batter to another bowl, and sieve in the cocoa powder. Stir until combined. Alternate spoonfuls of the chocolate batter and plain batter in the loaf tin, and then swirl the two together lightly and sparingly with a knife. Sprinkle with the chocolate chips and peanut butter chips. Bake for about an hour, until the bread is golden brown, well risen and a cocktail stick inserted into the centre comes out clean. Remove from the oven and cool in the tin for 10 minutes. Turn out to cool on a wire rack before slicing.

Makes 1 loaf

cranberry, raisin & hazelnut breakfast bread

see variations page 76

This loaf is moist and nutty, with succulent raisins and a hint of orange.

255 g (9 oz) plain flour
1 1/2 tsp baking powder
1 tsp bicarbonate of soda
1/2 tsp salt
85 g (3 oz) chopped toasted hazelnuts
85 g (3 oz) dried cranberries

85 g (3 oz) raisins
60 ml (2 fl oz) sunflower oil
1 egg, room temperature
180 ml (6 fl oz) orange juice
170 g (6 oz) sugar
butter for greasing

Preheat oven to 180°C (350°F) and grease a 450 g (1 lb) 20 x 10-cm (8 x 4-in) loaf tin with a little butter. Dust the tin lightly with flour. In a large bowl, sieve together the flour, baking powder, bicarbonate of soda and salt. Add the hazelnuts, cranberries and raisins, and stir until the nuts and fruit are well coated with flour.

In a small bowl, whisk the oil and egg together, and in another bowl, mix the orange juice and sugar together. Make a well in the centre of the flour, add both the egg mixture and the orange juice mixture, and stir quickly and lightly until the batter is just blended. Pour the mixture into the tin and bake for about 50–55 minutes, until golden brown and a cocktail stick inserted into the centre comes out clean.

Makes 1 loaf

australian damper bread

see variations page 77

This traditional Australian outback bread is commonly cooked in a campfire, but it bakes just as well in your kitchen oven.

510 g (1 lb 2 oz) self-raising flour   355 (12 fl oz) milk
1/2 tsp salt   oil for greasing

Preheat the oven to 220°C (425°F) and lightly oil a 20-cm (8-in) round baking tin. In a large bowl, sieve the flour and salt together and make a well in the centre. Add the milk, and mix until well blended to make a soft but not sticky dough. If the dough feels too dry, add a little extra milk, and if it feels too wet, add a little extra flour.

Transfer the dough to the baking tin, and make a cross in the top. Bake for 30 minutes, or until golden brown and the bottom of the loaf sounds hollow when tapped.

Makes 1 loaf

variations

maple pecan breakfast bread

see base recipe page 51

maple pecan breakfast bread with bourbon icing
Prepare the basic recipe. Whisk together 3 tablespoons melted butter, 2–3 teaspoons bourbon and 125 g (4^1/$_2$ oz) sieved icing sugar. Add enough milk to make a fairly stiff icing and spread over cooled bread. Sprinkle with chopped candied ginger.

peach & pecan breakfast bread
Prepare the basic recipe, replacing 2 bananas with 2 stoned, chopped fresh peaches.

nutty carrot & cinnamon bread
Prepare the basic recipe, replacing 3 bananas and the pecans with 180 g (6^1/$_4$ oz) finely grated carrots and 125 g (4^1/$_2$ oz) chopped walnuts. Add 1 teaspoon cinnamon to the mixture.

maple pecan bread with streusel topping
Prepare the basic recipe, omitting the pecan topping. In a medium bowl, combine 75 g (2^1/$_2$ oz) brown sugar, 2 tablespoons flour, 1 tablespoon melted butter, and 40 g (1^1/$_2$ oz) chopped pecans, and sprinkle evenly over batter in tin.

variations

hot cinnamon ring

see base recipe page 52

hot ginger & pistachio ring
Prepare the basic recipe, replacing the cinnamon and almonds with ground ginger and chopped pistachios.

hot apple cinnamon ring
Prepare the basic recipe. While making the syrup, add 2 peeled, cored and finely chopped apples to the pan, and cook over a gentle heat for 3 minutes. Cool and proceed as directed.

hot cherry & almond ring
Prepare the basic recipe, replacing the pecans with dried cherries.

hot apple & raisin ring
Prepare the basic recipe, adding 2 peeled, cored and finely chopped apples to the syrup as above. Replace the pecans and almonds with 125 g (4½ oz) raisins.

variations

fruity malt loaf

see base recipe page 54

cherry & macadamia nut malt loaf
Prepare the basic recipe, replacing the sultanas with 85 g (3 oz) dried cherries and 40 g
(1½ oz) chopped macadamia nuts.

coconut & pineapple malt loaf
Prepare the basic recipe, replacing the golden raisins with 25 g (⅔ oz) flaked coconut and
60 g (2 oz) chopped candied or freeze-dried pineapple.

cranberry malt loaf with white chocolate glaze
Prepare the basic recipe, replacing the sultanas with dried cranberries. In a microwave-safe
bowl, melt 40 g (1½ oz) white chocolate buttons on medium power until smooth. Stir in
3 tablespoons icing sugar and enough French vanilla liquid coffee creamer to make a slightly
runny icing. Drizzle over cooled loaf.

ginger malt loaf
Prepare the basic recipe, adding 1 teaspoon ground ginger and 40 g (1½ oz) chopped
candied ginger to the flour.

variations

jam doughnuts

see base recipe page 55

doughnut sticks with chocolate dipping sauce
Prepare the basic recipe. Shape the doughnuts into sticks rather than balls and proceed as directed. Stir together 75 g (2½ oz) dark chocolate chips, 2 tablespoons milk chocolate chips, 1 tablespoon golden syrup and 160 ml (5 fl oz) double cream in a pan over low heat until the chocolate has melted and the sauce is smooth. Serve on the side for dipping.

jam doughnuts with strawberry & white chocolate
Prepare the basic recipe. Fill with strawberry jam. Mix 125 g (4½ oz) sieved icing sugar with just enough milk to make a smooth, fairly stiff icing. Add ½ teaspoon glycerin (keeps the icing soft) and a little pink food colouring, and spread over the doughnuts while they are still warm. Dot each one with white chocolate chips.

jam doughnuts with cream
Prepare the basic recipe. Split the doughnut in half horizontally. Spread one half with strawberry jam, add whipped cream and top with the other half of the doughnut.

cherry & vanilla glazed doughnuts
Prepare the basic recipe, replacing the strawberry or raspberry jam with black cherry jam. Glaze with soft icing (see page 236), with 1 teaspoon vanilla extract added to the icing.

variations

orange & cinnamon swirl bread

see base recipe page 56

orange & cinnamon-raisin swirl bread
Prepare the basic recipe, adding 340 g (12 oz) raisins to the bowl with the flour.

orange & cinnamon swirl bread with orange marmalade glaze
Prepare the basic recipe. In a small pan, heat 250 g (9 oz) orange marmalade with
2 teaspoons water until runny enough to brush over the warm bread.

olive & anchovy swirl bread
Prepare the basic recipe, omitting the 3 tablespoons sugar and orange from the bread recipe.
Replace the filling with a small bunch of basil (thick stalks removed), 340 g (12 oz) pitted
black olives, 4 tinned anchovies and 5 tablespoons olive oil, blended together in a mini-
processor or with a hand blender.

cheese & garlic swirl bread
Prepare the basic recipe, omitting the 3 tablespoons sugar and orange from the bread recipe.
Replace the filling with 110 g (4 oz) butter mixed with 3 crushed cloves of garlic, and 120 g
(4 oz) each of grated mozzarella and cheddar cheese.

variations

chocolate–pistachio espresso bread

see base recipe page 59

coffee-glazed chocolate–pistachio espresso bread
Prepare the basic recipe. Make glaze by beating 115 g (4 oz) icing sugar with just enough very strong coffee to make a smooth icing. Spread over warm loaf.

butterscotch & chocolate–pistachio espresso bread
Prepare the basic recipe, adding 55 g (2 oz) butterscotch chips with the pistachio nuts.

coffee-bean pistachio espresso bread
Prepare the basic recipe, adding 85 g (3 oz) chocolate-covered coffee beans (chopped in half) with the pistachio nuts.

chocolate–hazelnut espresso bread
Prepare the basic recipe, replacing the pistachio nuts with toasted and chopped hazelnuts.

variations

light & flaky croissants

see base recipe page 60

almond croissants
Prepare the basic recipe, spreading each croissant with frangipane made by mixing 60 g (2 oz) butter with 50 g (1¾ oz) sugar, 1 egg, 30 g (1 oz) flour, ¼ teaspoon baking powder, 50 g (1¾ oz) ground almonds and ½ teaspoon almond extract. Roll as directed.

chocolate croissants
Prepare the basic recipe, and just before rolling up, place a small square of chocolate at the wide edge of the triangle.

tapenade, thyme & goat's cheese croissants
Prepare the basic recipe. Make filling by mixing together 85 g (3 oz) goat's cheese, 40 g (1½ oz) chopped pitted black olives and ½ teaspoon dried thyme. Spread each croissant with filling just before rolling.

chocolate-hazelnut croissants
Prepare the basic recipe, spreading each croissant with chocolate-hazelnut spread before rolling.

variations

brioche

see base recipe page 62

lemon & raisin brioche
Prepare the basic recipe, adding the zest of 1 lemon and 85 g (3 oz) raisins to the flour.

chocolate chip & orange brioche
Prepare the basic recipe, adding 75 g (2½ oz) dark chocolate chips, 1 teaspoon pure orange extract and the zest of 1 orange to the flour with the eggs.

braided brioche with chocolate bars
Prepare the basic recipe. Roll the dough out to a 38 x 23-cm (15 x 9-in) rectangle and arrange a line of chocolate bars (such as Snickers) down the centre. Make cuts diagonally between the chocolate and the edge of the dough down each side, and fold them up over the chocolate bars like a lattice. Brush with egg white and bake in preheated oven at 190°C (375°F) for 20–25 minutes, until golden brown.

cinnamon & cherry brioche
Prepare the basic recipe, adding 2 teaspoons cinnamon and 85 g (3 oz) dried cherries to the bowl with the flour.

chocolate & peanut butter bread

see base recipe page 63

chocolate & peanut butter bread with chocolate glaze
Prepare the basic recipe, omitting the topping. Make glaze by melting 60 g (2 oz) milk chocolate with 1 tablespoon milk in a bowl over a pan of barely simmering water. Stir until smooth, cool, and drizzle over cooled bread.

white chocolate & peanut butter bread
Prepare the basic recipe, replacing the dark chocolate chips with white chocolate chips.

chocolate & raisin-peanut butter bread
Prepare the basic recipe, adding 85 g (3 oz) raisins to the flour.

chocolate courgette bread
Prepare the basic recipe, replacing the bananas, peanut butter chips and peanut butter with 175 g (6 oz) finely grated courgette and 50 g (1¾ oz) milk chocolate chips.

variations

cranberry, raisin & hazelnut breakfast bread

see base recipe page 65

cherry, raisin & macadamia nut breakfast bread
Prepare the basic recipe, replacing the cranberries and hazelnuts with dried cherries and chopped macadamia nuts.

raspberry, raisin & walnut breakfast bread
Prepare the basic recipe, replacing the cranberries and hazelnuts with fresh raspberries and chopped walnuts.

mango, raisin & pecan breakfast bread
Prepare the basic recipe, replacing the cranberries and hazelnuts with chopped fresh mango and chopped pecans.

blueberry, sultana & white chocolate chip bread
Prepare the basic recipe, replacing the cranberries, raisins and hazelnuts with fresh blueberries, sultanas and white chocolate chips.

variations

australian damper bread

see base recipe page 66

buttermilk, raisin & sultana australian damper bread
Prepare the basic recipe, replacing 120 ml (4 fl oz) milk with 120 ml (4 fl oz) buttermilk.
Add 125 g (4½ oz) raisins and 125 g (4½ oz) sultanas to the bowl with the flour.

almond australian damper bread
Prepare the basic recipe, adding 60 g (2 oz) chopped almonds to the bowl with the flour.

mozzarella australian damper bread
Prepare the basic recipe. Transfer half of the dough to the tin, place a 60-g (2-oz) piece of
mozzarella on the dough and put the rest of the dough on top. Bake as directed.

garlic & basil australian damper bread
Prepare the basic recipe, adding 2 crushed cloves of garlic and 15 g (⅔ oz) freshly chopped
basil to the bowl with the flour.

tea & coffee breads

Mid-morning or mid-afternoon, the feeling

is the same, and in this chapter you will find

energy-boosting bread recipes, quick and yeast-

based, to get you through to your next meal.

crumpets

see variations page 99

You will need crumpet rings or round metal biscuit cutters to make these teatime snacks. Toast the plain side first, the bubbly side second, and spread liberally with butter.

450 g (1 lb) plain flour
355 ml (12 fl oz) warm whole milk
355 ml (12 fl oz) warm water
2 tsp active dry yeast

2 tsp sugar
2 tsp salt
$\frac{1}{2}$ tsp bicarbonate of soda
sunflower oil for greasing

In a large bowl, whisk the flour, milk, warm water, yeast and sugar into a runny batter the consistency of single cream. Cover with cling film and leave at room temperature until really bubbly. This could take an hour or more.

Heat a heavy-based frying pan or flat griddle over a medium-high heat. Whisk the salt and bicarbonate of soda into the batter. Lightly grease the crumpet rings and pan with a little sunflower oil. Put one ring into the pan and fill to just below the top of the ring with some batter. If it oozes out underneath, whisk a little more flour in, as it is too runny. If it fails to produce lots of holes within a minute or two, add a little more water, as it is too thick. When the consistency is right, the crumpets will be ready to flip over in the rings after about 4–5 minutes. Cook the other side for 2–3 minutes. If they brown too much too fast, turn the heat down slightly. Repeat until all the batter has been used. Either serve immediately, or cool on a wire rack and toast later.

Makes 12 crumpets

sally lunn tea bread

see variations page 100

This is the original Bath bun, invented in the seventeenth century by a Frenchwoman in Bath, southwest England.

205 ml (7 fl oz) + 2 tbsp warm whole milk
50 g (2 oz) butter + extra for greasing
2 tsp + 1 tbsp sugar, divided
2 tsp active dry yeast

450 g (1 lb) white bread flour
1 tsp salt
2 eggs, room temperature, lightly beaten
1 tbsp water

Lightly grease two 15-cm (6-in) round cake tins with a little butter. In a small pan over a gentle heat, warm the milk and butter together until the butter has just melted. Dissolve 2 teaspoons sugar in the warm milk and butter, sprinkle the yeast on top and leave for 10–15 minutes until frothy. In a large bowl, sieve together the flour and salt. Make a well in the centre and add the yeast liquid and eggs. Gradually incorporate the flour into the liquid until a dough forms and it leaves the sides of the bowl clean. Turn out on to a lightly floured work surface and knead for about 10 minutes, until the dough is soft, smooth and elastic. Divide the dough into two pieces, gather each piece into a ball and place in a cake tin. Place each tin into a greased plastic bag, and put in a warm place for an hour or so, or until the dough has risen almost to the top of the tins. Preheat the oven to 230°C (450°F). Bake the bread for 15–20 minutes, until golden brown and the bottom of the loaves sound hollow when tapped. While the loaves are baking, make the topping by heating the remaining sugar and water together in a small pan over a low heat until the sugar has dissolved. Increase the heat to medium-high, bring to the boil and boil rapidly for 1–2 minutes. Turn the Sally Lunns out on to a wire rack to cool, and brush the tops with the sugar syrup while they are still warm.

Makes 2 loaves

fruity apple tea bread

see variations page 101

This is a quick autumn-spiced bread, sweetened with apples and sultanas, and topped with caramelised apples.

125 g (4½ oz) + 2 tbsp
   butter + extra for greasing
125 g (4½ oz) brown sugar
255 g (9 oz) sultanas
160 ml (5 fl oz) apple juice

2 apples, peeled and cored
2 eggs, room temperature,
   lightly beaten
285 g (10 oz) plain flour
1 tsp cinnamon

1 tsp ground ginger
2 tsp bicarbonate of soda
½ tsp baking powder
2 tsp lemon juice
2 tbsp maple syrup

Preheat the oven to 180°C (350°F). Lightly butter a 900 g (2 lb) 23 x 13-cm (9 x 5-in) loaf tin and line the base with baking paper. In a small pan over a gentle heat, warm the butter, sugar, sultanas and apple juice, until the butter has melted. Pour into a medium bowl and set aside to cool. Chop one of the apples and add to the bowl with the beaten eggs, and sieve the flour, cinnamon, ginger, bicarbonate of soda and baking powder over the apple mixture. Stir lightly and quickly until just combined, transfer to the loaf tin and smooth the top.

To make the topping, slice the remaining apple, toss in the lemon juice and arrange on top of the mixture. Bake in the oven for 45–50 minutes, or until a toothpick inserted into the centre comes out clean. Check halfway through and cover the top with aluminium foil if the apples are browning too much. Leave to cool in the tin for 10 minutes before turning out on to a wire rack to cool. Brush the top with maple syrup while still warm. Serve warm or cold.

Makes 1 loaf

white chocolate & cherry teacakes

see variations page 102

Although not strictly bread, teacakes make afternoons complete – and this recipe is heavenly.

515 g (13$^1/_2$ oz) plain flour
1 tbsp baking powder
$^1/_4$ tsp salt
50 g (2 oz) sugar
170 g (6 oz) dried cherries

100 g (4 oz) chopped white chocolate
475 ml (16 fl oz) whipping cream
milk for brushing
coarse sugar for sprinkling

Preheat the oven to 220°C (425°F) and line a large baking sheet with baking paper. In a medium bowl, sieve the flour, baking powder and salt. Add the sugar, cherries and white chocolate, and toss to combine. Add the cream and stir until the dough comes together. On a lightly floured surface, knead the dough a few times and pat it out gently to about 2.5 cm (1 in) thick.

With a 6.5-cm (2$^1/_2$-in) cutter, cut the dough into 10 teacakes. Transfer on to the baking sheet. Brush the tops with a little milk and sprinkle with coarse sugar. Bake for 15–20 minutes, or until golden. Transfer to a wire rack to cool, and serve warm.

Makes 10 teacakes

chelsea buns

see variations page 103

These buns are a perfect accompaniment to morning coffee, full of sugar and dried fruit.

½ tsp sugar, dissolved in 160 ml (5 fl oz) warm whole milk
2 tsp active dry yeast
250 g (9 oz) white bread flour, divided
½ tsp salt

2 eggs, room temperature, lightly beaten
25 g (1 oz) butter, melted + extra for brushing
85 g (3 oz) brown sugar
85 g (3 oz) mixed dried fruit

2 tbsp candied orange peel, chopped
1 tsp cinnamon
honey for glazing
oil for greasing

Lightly oil a 20-cm (8-in) square baking tin. Sprinkle the yeast on top of the sugar–milk mix, stir in 65 g (2¼ oz) flour, and leave for about 25 minutes, until frothy. In a large bowl, sieve together the remaining flour and salt, make a well in the centre and pour in the yeast liquid. Add the eggs and melted butter, and mix well until a dough comes together. On a lightly floured work surface, knead the dough using your hands and knuckles for about 10 minutes, until the dough is soft, smooth and elastic. Transfer the dough to a large lightly oiled bowl, and turn to coat it all over. Cover and put in a warm place for an hour or so, until doubled in size. Turn the dough out on to a lightly floured work surface, knock back and knead the dough again for 2 minutes. Roll the dough out to a 23 x 30-cm (9 x 12-in) rectangle. Brush with a little butter, and sprinkle on the brown sugar, mixed dried fruit, orange peel and cinnamon. Roll up tightly like a Swiss roll and seal the edge. Cut into nine slices and lay in the baking tin, cut side down. Leave to rise until the dough feels springy, about 30 minutes. Preheat the oven to 190°C (375°F). Remove the plastic bag and bake for 30–35 minutes, until golden brown. Remove the buns to a wire rack to cool, and brush with honey while still warm.

Makes 9 buns

german apple kuchen

see variations page 104

This is an enriched yeast dough topped with sliced apples, brushed with butter and sprinkled with sugar and cinnamon.

120 ml (4 fl oz) whole milk
225 g (8 oz) + 2 tbsp sugar
60 ml (2 fl oz) warm water
2 tsp active dry yeast
2 tbsp butter, softened
1 egg, room temperature
255 g (9 oz) plain flour
1 tsp salt

450 g (1 lb) eating apples, peeled, cored and sliced

for the topping
225 g (8 oz) sugar
2 tsp + 1/2 tsp cinnamon, divided
2 tsp butter, softened + extra for greasing
1 egg yolk, room temperature
60 ml (2 fl oz) single cream

Butter a 33 x 23-cm (13 x 9-in) baking dish. In a small pan over a medium heat, heat the milk until just below boiling, remove from heat and set aside. Dissolve the sugar in the warm water, sprinkle the yeast on top and leave for 10–15 minutes until frothy. When the milk has cooled to lukewarm, mix with the yeast mixture, butter and egg, and beat until blended. Gradually add flour and salt to form a batter. Cover and let rise until doubled in size, about an hour or so. Pour the batter into the baking dish. Butter your fingers to prevent them sticking, and use them to spread the batter evenly. Arrange the apple slices on top of the batter. Cover and put in a warm place to rise again, about 30 minutes. Preheat the oven to 190°C (375°F). Bake the kuchen for 20 minutes. Mix all of the topping ingredients together. Remove the kuchen from the oven and pour over topping. Return to the oven and bake for another 15–20 minutes. Remove from the oven and allow to stand for 15 minutes before serving warm.

Makes 6 servings

french beignets

see variations page 105

These divine doughnuts should be drenched in sugar and served hot with milky coffee.

2 tsp active dry yeast
100 g (4 oz) sugar
2 tbsp white vegetable fat
300 ml (10 fl oz) warm whole milk
1 egg, room temperature

570 g (1 lb 4 oz) plain flour
pinch of salt
icing sugar for dusting
oil for greasing

In the bowl of a stand mixer with a dough hook attachment, beat together the yeast, sugar, vegetable fat and milk. After 2–3 minutes, add the egg and mix again for 1 minute. Add the flour and the salt, and beat at low speed until all the flour has been incorporated and the dough forms a ball, leaves the sides of the bowl, and starts to climb up the dough hook. Gather the dough into a smooth ball and place it in a large lightly oiled bowl. Turn it around to coat it all over, cover and put in a warm place for about 2 hours, until doubled in size.

Preheat a deep-fat fryer to 182°C (360°F). Turn the dough out on to a lightly floured work surface and pat the dough into a rectangle about 2.5 cm (1 in) thick. Roll it out to 31 x 25 cm (12$\frac{1}{2}$ x 10 in), and 6 mm ($\frac{1}{4}$ in) thick. With a sharp knife, cut the dough into twenty 6.5-cm (2$\frac{1}{2}$-in) squares. Fry them in batches for 3–5 minutes, until golden brown and crispy on all sides. Remove from the fryer and drain on paper towels. Transfer to a wire rack, dust liberally with icing sugar and serve hot or warm.

Makes 20 beignets

yorkshire teacakes

see variations page 106

These little fruit buns should be split, toasted and generously spread with butter for a delicious morning or afternoon snack. Enjoy with a cup of tea.

1 tsp + 2 tbsp sugar, divided
300 ml (10 fl oz) warm whole milk
2 tsp active dry yeast
450 g (1 lb) white bread flour

1 tsp salt
2 tbsp butter + extra for greasing
55 g (2 oz) dried currants

Lightly grease a large baking sheet with a little butter. In a small bowl, dissolve 1 teaspoon sugar in the warm milk, sprinkle the yeast on top and leave for 10–15 minutes until frothy. In a large bowl, sieve the flour and salt together. Add the remaining 2 tablespoons sugar and cut in the butter until the mixture resembles fine breadcrumbs. Stir in the currants. Make a well in the centre of the flour mixture and pour in the yeast liquid. Mix the ingredients together, beating the dough against the side of the bowl until it leaves the sides clean. Turn the dough out on to a lightly floured work surface and knead for about 10 minutes until the dough is soft, smooth and elastic. Put the dough in a lightly oiled bowl and turn to coat it all over. Cover and leave in a warm place for an hour or so until doubled in size. Turn the dough out on to a lightly floured work surface and punch down. Knead for 3–4 minutes, then divide the dough into six equal pieces. Form each piece into a ball and roll out to about 1.5-cm (1/2-in)-thick cakes. Place well apart on the baking sheet and brush the tops with a little milk. Place the baking sheet in an oiled plastic bag and leave to rise in a warm place for about 45 minutes, until doubled in size. Preheat the oven to 200°C (400°F). Bake the teacakes for 20 minutes, until golden brown. Cool on a wire rack.

Makes 6 teacakes

soft pretzels

see variations page 107

Those soft pretzels you can buy in American malls are so delicious – these are very similar, and easy to make yourself.

1 tsp + 100 g (4 oz) sugar, divided
4 tsp active dry yeast
300 ml (10 fl oz) + 1 l (2 pints) warm water, divided
500 g (1 lb 2 oz) plain flour

1 1/2 tsp salt
1 tbsp oil
polenta for dusting
60 g (2 oz) bicarbonate of soda

Line three or four large baking sheets with baking paper, and dust with fine polenta. Dissolve 1 teaspoon sugar in 300 ml (10 fl oz) warm water, sprinkle the yeast on top and leave for 10–15 minutes until frothy. In a large bowl, mix the flour, remaining 100 g (4 oz) sugar and salt together. Make a well in the centre, pour in the yeast liquid and 1 tablespoon oil and mix until a dough begins to form. Knead for about 10 minutes to make a smooth, soft and silky dough. Transfer the dough to a lightly oiled bowl and turn to coat it all over. Cover and put in a warm place for an hour or so, until doubled in size. Turn the dough out on to a lightly floured work surface, punch down and knead for 1 minute to expel the air. Divide the dough into 12 equal pieces and form into logs. Leave to rest for 10 minutes. Roll each piece vertically between your hands into a long, thin rope, and twist into a pretzel shape. Place the pretzels on the baking sheets, cover with cling film and chill in the fridge for 30 minutes, or overnight. Preheat the oven to 200°C (400°F). Prepare a water bath by dissolving the bicarbonate of soda in the remaining hot water in a large bowl. Dip each pretzel into the water bath and place back on the baking sheet. Sprinkle with coarse salt and bake for 8 minutes. Remove from the oven and leave to cool on a wire rack, or serve hot.

Makes 12 pretzels

alli's favourite monkey bread

see variations page 108

This delectable orange-glazed, pull-apart bread was the absolute winner with my friend and neighbour, Alli. It is traditionally baked in a tube tin, but I prefer a round cake tin.

for the glaze
5 tbsp butter
3 tbsp orange juice
40 g (1½ oz) brown sugar

for the dough
1 tsp white sugar
300 ml (10 fl oz) whole milk
2 tsp instant dry yeast
450 g (1 lb) white bread flour
1 tsp salt

for coating
1 tbsp cinnamon
200 g (8 oz) sugar

oil for greasing

Grease a large round cake tin (preferably not springform because it might leak) with a little oil. To make the glaze, over a medium heat, melt the butter in a small pan with the juice, add the brown sugar and stir to dissolve. In a small bowl, mix the cinnamon and sugar for the coating.

To make the dough, dissolve the sugar in the warm milk, sprinkle the yeast on top and leave for 10–15 minutes until frothy. In a large bowl, mix flour and salt. Make a well in the centre, add the yeast liquid and work to a soft dough. If the mixture seems too dry, add a little extra water, and if it seems too wet, add a little extra flour. Turn out on to a lightly floured work surface and knead for about 10 minutes until it is soft, smooth and elastic. Turn the dough out on to a lightly floured work surface, form into a thick log and cut into about 32 pieces. Roll quickly into balls. Dip each ball in the glaze and then roll in the cinnamon sugar. Start layering the balls in the tin, leaving room on the bottom layer for the balls to expand as they rise. They should be close, but not touching. On each successive layer, place balls so that they overlap

empty spaces underneath. When you have used up all the balls, pour any remaining glaze over the top and sprinkle on the remaining cinnamon sugar. Cover and leave to rise at room temperature for about 1½ hours, until doubled in size. Preheat the oven to 170°C (325°F). Remove cover and bake for about 25–30 minutes, until browned. Leave to cool in the tin for 5 minutes. Invert bread on to a serving plate, being careful of the hot syrup, and cool slightly before serving.

Makes 6 servings

devonshire splits

see variations page 109

So called because, just like a Devonshire scone, these are filled with cream and strawberry jam.

450 g (1 lb) plain flour
1/2 tsp salt
1 tsp sugar
60 ml (2 fl oz) warm milk
4 tsp active dry yeast

1 tbsp butter
60 ml (2 fl oz) warm water
oil for greasing
strawberry jam, to serve
clotted or whipped double cream, to serve

Grease two large baking sheets with a little oil. In a large bowl, mix the flour and salt together. Dissolve the sugar in the warm milk, sprinkle the yeast on top and leave for 10–15 minutes until frothy. Melt the butter in the warm water. Make a well in the centre of the flour and add the yeast liquid and melted butter mixture. Mix until a dough forms. Knead for 10 minutes, until the dough is soft, smooth and elastic. Place the dough in a large lightly oiled bowl and turn to coat it all over. Cover and leave in a warm place for an hour or so, until doubled in size. Turn the dough out on to a lightly floured work surface, punch down and divide into 12 pieces. Form each piece into a ball, turning it around on the work surface and tucking the sides under as you go, and flatten into a round 1.5 cm (1/2 in) thick. Place on the baking sheets, place inside an oiled plastic bag and leave to rise again in a warm place for 20 minutes. Preheat the oven to 230°C (450°F). Brush the buns with milk and bake for 15 minutes. Remove from the oven and cool on a wire rack.

To finish, cut each bun almost in half and spread with jam and cream.

Makes 12 splits

raspberry & almond tea bread

see variations page 110

This is a fresh-tasting quick bread, full of the flavour of raspberries, the crunch of almonds and a faint tang of lemon.

50 g (2 oz) butter + extra for greasing
200 g (8 oz) sugar
1 egg, room temperature
160 ml (5 fl oz) whole milk
190 g (7 oz) plain flour

1 tsp baking powder
1 tsp cinnamon
100 g (4 oz) fresh or frozen raspberries
50 g (2 oz) sliced almonds
2 tsp finely grated lemon zest

Preheat the oven to 180°C (350°F) and lightly grease a 450-g (1-lb) 20 x 10-cm (8 x 4-in) loaf tin with a little butter. In a large bowl, with an electric hand mixer, whisk the butter and sugar until light and creamy. Add the egg and the milk, and whisk again until well mixed. Sieve the flour, baking powder and cinnamon into the bowl, and fold together. Add the raspberries, almonds and lemon zest, and fold again, until just combined. Transfer to the loaf tin, smooth the top and bake for 60–70 minutes, until golden brown and a cocktail stick inserted into the centre comes out clean. Leave to cool in the tin for 5 minutes before turning out to cool on a wire rack.

Makes 6 servings

quick gluten-free cinnamon bread

see variations page 111

If you have a favourite brand of gluten-free flour, you could substitute 190 g (7 oz) for
the rice flour, tapioca flour and potato starch.

50 g (2 oz) sugar
160 ml (5 fl oz) warm milk
4 tsp active dry yeast
140 g (5 oz) rice flour
25 g (1 oz) tapioca flour
25 g (1 oz) potato starch
$^{1}/_{2}$ tsp xanthan gum

$^{1}/_{2}$ tsp baking powder
$^{1}/_{2}$ tsp cinnamon
$^{1}/_{4}$ tsp salt
1 egg, room temperature,
    lightly beaten
butter for greasing

for the topping
3 tbsp butter, softened
100 g (4 oz) brown sugar
$1^{1}/_{2}$ tsp cinnamon

Lightly butter a 20 x 20-cm (8 x 8-in) baking tin. Dissolve the sugar in the warm milk, sprinkle
the yeast on top and leave for 10–15 minutes until frothy. In a large bowl, whisk the rice flour,
tapioca flour, potato starch, xanthan gum, baking powder, cinnamon and salt together. Make
a well in the centre, pour in the yeast liquid and egg and beat with an electric hand mixer
to form a thick batter. Pour into the baking tin, cover and put in a warm place for an hour or
so, until almost doubled in size.

In a medium bowl, mix the butter with the brown sugar and cinnamon so that it forms
clumps. Sprinkle the topping over the dough, pushing some down into it. Preheat the oven
to 180°C (350°F). Bake for 25–35 minutes, or until a cocktail stick inserted into the centre
comes out clean. Remove from the oven and cool in the pan for 10 minutes. Turn out on to
a wire rack to cool.

Makes 8 servings

crumpets

see base recipe page 79

crumpets with raisins
Prepare the basic recipe, adding 170 g (6 oz) raisins to the flour.

crumpets with cheese & onion topping
Prepare the basic recipe. Mix 170 g (6 oz) grated cheddar cheese with 1 teaspoon Dijon mustard, 2 thinly sliced spring onions and 1 beaten egg. Spread on the crumpets and grill for 3–4 minutes, until golden brown and the egg is cooked.

cherry crumpets
Prepare the basic recipe, adding 170 g (6 oz) dried cherries to the flour.

cheesy bacon & egg crumpets
Prepare the basic recipe. Cook 12 rashers of bacon until crispy. Cut in half. Top each crumpet with 1 teaspoon caramelised onion chutney, 4 cherry tomato halves and 30 g (1 oz) grated cheddar cheese. Grill for 3–4 minutes until the cheese is golden. Top each with 2 pieces of bacon, a poached egg and a sprinkling of chopped parsley.

variations

sally lunn tea bread

see base recipe page 80

sultana sally lunn tea bread
Prepare the basic recipe, adding 170 g (6 oz) sultanas to the flour.

sally lunn bundt with pecan topping
Prepare the basic recipe. Mix together 100 g (4 oz) dark brown sugar, 100 g (4 oz) melted unsalted butter, and 75 g (2½ oz) chopped pecans, and spoon into the bottom of a large greased bundt tin. Add the dough and bake in a preheated oven at 180°C (350°F) for 40 minutes. Invert on to a serving plate.

chocolate sally lunn tea bread
Prepare the basic recipe, adding 150 g (6 oz) dark chocolate chips to the flour.

apricot & walnut sally lunn tea bread
Prepare the basic recipe, adding 115 g (4½ oz) chopped dried ready-to-eat apricots and 85 g (3 oz) chopped walnuts to the flour.

variations

fruity apple tea bread

see base recipe page 83

blackberry & apple tea bread
Prepare the basic recipe, replacing 85 g (3 oz) sultanas with 170 g (6 oz) fresh blackberries.

glazed fruity apple tea bread
Prepare the basic recipe, omitting the maple syrup topping. Make glaze by mixing 125 g (4½ oz) sieved icing sugar with enough lemon juice to make a runny icing. Drizzle over the top of the cooled loaf.

blueberry & apple tea bread
Prepare the basic recipe, replacing 85 g (3 oz) sultanas with 170 g (6 oz) fresh blueberries.

fruity apple & ginger tea bread
Prepare the basic recipe, replacing 85 g (3 oz) sultanas with 85 g (3 oz) chopped candied ginger.

tea & coffee breads   101

variations

white chocolate & cherry teacakes

see base recipe page 84

sultana & ginger teacakes
Prepare the basic recipe, replacing the cherries and white chocolate with 85 g (3 oz) sultanas. Add 2 teaspoons ground ginger to the flour mix.

date & coconut teacakes
Prepare the basic recipe, replacing the cherries and white chocolate with 170 g (6 oz) stoned, chopped, dried ready-to-eat dates and 25 g (1¾ oz) flaked coconut.

lemon & currant teacakes
Prepare the basic recipe, replacing the cherries and white chocolate with 170 g (6 oz) currants. Add the zest of 1 lemon to the flour mix.

cheese & whole-kernel corn teacakes
Prepare the basic recipe, replacing the cherries and white chocolate with 125 g (4½ oz) grated cheddar cheese and 125 g (4½ oz) whole-kernel corn.

variations

chelsea buns

see base recipe page 85

belgian buns
Prepare the basic recipe. Glaze with soft icing (see cinnamon buns recipe page 252).

cranberry & apricot buns
Prepare the basic recipe, replacing the mixed dried fruit in the filling with 125 g (4½ oz) dried cranberries and 40 g (1½ oz) chopped, dried ready-to-eat apricots.

chocolate chip & cherry buns
Prepare the basic recipe, replacing the dried fruit with 85 g (3 oz) dried cherries and 85 g (3 oz) dark chocolate chips.

date & walnut buns
Prepare the basic recipe, omitting the dried fruit and substituting 85 g (3 oz) chopped, dried ready-to-eat dates and 60 g (2 oz) chopped walnuts.

variations

german apple kuchen

see base recipe page 86

cherry kuchen
Prepare the basic recipe, replacing the apples with one 400-g (14-oz) tin cherry pie filling.

apple & blackberry kuchen
Prepare the basic recipe, replacing 150 g (5½ oz) apples with 150 g (5½ oz) fresh blackberries. Sprinkle 1 tablespoon sugar on top.

peach & brown sugar kuchen
Prepare the basic recipe, replacing the apples with fresh peach slices, and sprinkling 2 tablespoons dark brown sugar on top.

raspberry & almond kuchen
Prepare the basic recipe, replacing the apple topping with a layer of frangipane (see croissant variation recipe page 73). Top with raspberries and proceed as directed.

french beignets

see base recipe page 88

french beignets with chocolate dipping sauce
Prepare the basic recipe. Make a chocolate dipping sauce (see doughnut variation recipe page 70) and serve on the side.

raisin beignets
Prepare the basic recipe and add 170 g (6 oz) raisins to the flour.

chocolate orange beignets
Prepare the basic recipe, adding the zest of 1 orange, 1 teaspoon pure orange extract and 150 g (5½ oz) dark chocolate chips to the flour with the milk.

hot chocolate with whipped cream
Prepare the basic recipe and serve with hot chocolate. For 6 servings, heat 100 g (4 oz) sugar and 120 ml (4 fl oz) water until the sugar dissolves. Simmer for 2 minutes, add 130 g (5 oz) good-quality dark chocolate and stir until melted. Whisk in 85 g (3 oz) unsweetened cocoa powder, 300 ml (5 fl oz) single cream and 1 l (2 pints) whole milk. When hot, serve topped with whipped cream.

variations

yorkshire teacakes

see base recipe page 89

cranberry teacakes
Prepare the basic recipe, replacing the currants with dried cranberries and 1/2 teaspoon dried nutmeg.

cherry & sultana teacakes
Prepare the basic recipe, replacing the currants with 40 g (1 1/2 oz) dried cherries, 40 g (1 1/2 oz) sultanas and 1 teaspoon cinnamon.

date & ginger teacakes
Prepare the basic recipe, replacing the currants with chopped, dried ready-to-eat dates. Add 1 teaspoon ground ginger to the flour.

prune & pecan teacakes
Prepare the basic recipe, replacing the currants with 40 g (1 1/2 oz) stoned, chopped prunes and 40 g (1 1/2 oz) chopped pecans.

variations

soft pretzels

see base recipe page 91

cinnamon sugar pretzels
Prepare the basic recipe. Brush with melted butter while still hot from the oven, and roll in
100 g (4 oz) sugar mixed with 1 teaspoon cinnamon.

chocolate-dipped pretzels
Prepare the basic recipe. Brush with melted butter while still hot from the oven, roll in
cinnamon sugar and serve chocolate sauce for dipping on the side (see doughnut variation
recipe page 70).

jalapeño pretzels
Prepare the basic recipe. Just before baking, lay seeded and finely sliced jalapeños across the
top of each pretzel.

parmesan pretzels
Prepare the basic recipe. Brush with melted butter while still hot from the oven, and sprinkle
with finely grated Parmesan cheese.

variations

alli's favourite monkey bread

see base recipe page 92

pepperoni pizza monkey bread
Prepare the basic recipe, omitting the glaze and coating. Roll the balls out and place 1 slice pepperoni and 1 teaspoon mozzarella on each one. Enclose the dough around the filling. Roll the balls in 100 g (4 oz) melted butter mixed with 2 crushed cloves of garlic and 2 teaspoons oregano, and layer as directed. Bake and serve with pizza sauce for dipping (see salami pizza recipe page 149).

peanut butter monkey bread
Prepare the basic recipe. Omit the glaze, roll the dough in the sugar (no cinnamon) and drizzle 100 g (4 oz) warmed smooth peanut butter and 100 g (4 oz) warmed strawberry jam over the balls as you layer them in the tin. Drizzle 120 ml (4 fl oz) double cream over the monkey bread just before baking.

cranberry & orange monkey bread
Prepare the basic recipe, adding 170 g (6 oz) dried cranberries as you layer the balls.

garlic monkey bread
Prepare the basic recipe, omitting the orange glaze and cinnamon sugar coating. Roll each ball in 100 g (4 oz) melted butter mixed with 2 crushed cloves of garlic, and 1/4 teaspoon each of dried rosemary, basil and sage. Pour over remaining butter mixture and bake as directed.

devonshire splits

see base recipe page 95

white, pink & lemon iced buns
Prepare the basic recipe, but form into sausage shapes instead of balls. Bake for 8–10 minutes. Glaze with icing made by mixing 300 g (10½ oz) sieved icing sugar with enough water to make a spreadable icing. Remove two thirds into two other bowls and colour one pink and one lemon. Spread the three icings on the buns and decorate with hundreds and thousands.

lemon & cream splits
Prepare the basic recipe, adding the zest of 1 lemon to the flour. Split and fill with lemon curd and whipped cream.

chocolate & chestnut cream splits
Prepare the basic recipe. Make the filling by heating 100 g (4 oz) chopped dark chocolate with 180 ml (6 fl oz) whipping cream until melted. Cool. Blend the chocolate cream with 200 g (7 oz) unsweetened chestnut purée, 1 tablespoon sugar and 2 tablespoons brandy in a food processor until smooth. Pipe or spread the filling on the split buns.

dulce de leche cream splits
Prepare the basic recipe. Split and fill with dulce de leche and whipped cream.

variations

raspberry & almond tea bread

see base recipe page 96

caramel apple tea bread
Prepare the basic recipe, replacing the raspberries with 170 g (6 oz) peeled, cored, finely chopped apple, and adding 60 g (2 oz) butterscotch chips to the mixture.

cherry & almond tea bread
Prepare the basic recipe, replacing the raspberries with fresh stoned, chopped cherries.

cranberry, white chocolate & almond tea bread
Prepare the basic recipe, replacing the raspberries with 85 g (3 oz) dried cranberries and 85 g (3 oz) white chocolate chips.

peach & pistachio tea bread
Prepare the basic recipe, replacing the raspberries and almonds with freshly chopped peaches and chopped pistachios. Drizzle the top of the cooled loaf with melted white chocolate.

quick gluten-free cinnamon bread

see base recipe page 98

quick gluten-free lemon & blueberry bread
Prepare the basic recipe, omitting the cinnamon. Substitute 1 teaspoon vanilla extract and add the zest of 1 lemon and 60 g (2 oz) fresh blueberries to the flour.

quick gluten-free strawberry & macadamia nut bread
Prepare the basic recipe, adding 60 g (2 oz) hulled and chopped fresh strawberries (dried on kitchen paper) and 30 g (1 oz) chopped macadamia nuts to the flour.

quick gluten-free chocolate & chilli bread
Prepare the basic recipe, adding 75 g (2½ oz) dark chocolate chips and ¼ teaspoon crushed red chilli flakes to the flour.

quick gluten-free pineapple & coconut bread
Prepare the basic recipe, adding 60 g (2 oz) chopped fresh or tinned pineapple (dried on kitchen paper) and 20 g (¾ oz) flaked coconut to the bowl with the flour.

fruit, vegetable & nut breads

In this chapter, you will find inspiration from a
traditional banana and cranberry loaf to an olive
and sundried tomato loaf to exciting flavours such
as pear and cardamom.

banana & cranberry loaf

see variations page 130

Great any time of day, this loaf is not too sweet, and is delicious sliced, toasted and topped with caramelised apples.

190 g (7 oz) plain flour
30 g (1¼ oz) wholewheat flour
½ tsp salt
2 tsp baking powder
¼ tsp bicarbonate of soda
3 medium-size bananas (2 very ripe)

60 ml (2 fl oz) buttermilk
140 g (5 oz) butter
85 g (3 oz) sugar
2 eggs, room temperature, lightly beaten
85 g (3 oz) dried cranberries
oil for greasing

Preheat the oven to 180°C (350°F). Grease a 450-g (1-lb) 20 x 10-cm (8 x 4-in) loaf tin with oil and dust with flour. In a medium bowl, mix the flours, salt, baking powder and bicarbonate of soda together. In a separate bowl, mash the two very ripe bananas with the buttermilk. In a large bowl, beat the butter and the sugar together until creamy, with an electric hand mixer. Gradually add the beaten eggs to the creamed butter and sugar, beating continuously. Add the mashed bananas and the flour mix, and stir lightly. Do not over-mix. Slice the third banana, add it to the mixture with the cranberries and stir until just combined. Pour the batter into the loaf tin and bake for about 40 minutes, or until a cocktail stick inserted into the centre comes out clean. Leave to cool in the tin for 10 minutes before turning out on to a wire rack to cool.

Makes 1 loaf

broccoli bread

see variations page 131

This is a great way to use up leftover broccoli, and is very colourful, so it will be appetising to children.

2 tbsp vegetable oil, divided +
    extra for greasing
1 small onion, finely chopped
85 g (3 oz) plain flour
60 g (2 oz) fine polenta
2 tbsp sugar
1 tbsp baking powder

1 tsp salt
4 eggs, room temperature
50 g (2 oz) butter, melted
225 g (8 oz) ricotta cheese
40 g (1½ oz) chopped
    sundried tomatoes (well
    drained if in oil)

100 g (4 oz) fresh steamed
    broccoli florets, chopped
20 g (¾ oz) finely grated
    Parmesan cheese

Preheat the oven to 200°C (400°F) and lightly grease a 450-g (1-lb) 20 x 10-cm (8 x 4-in) loaf tin with a little oil. In a medium frying pan over a medium heat, add 1 tablespoon vegetable oil. When it is hot but not smoking, sauté the onion until softened, about 5 minutes. Set aside to cool.

In a large bowl, mix together the flour, polenta, sugar, baking powder and salt. In a medium bowl, whisk the eggs with the rest of the vegetable oil. Stir in the melted butter and the ricotta cheese. Add the sundried tomatoes, broccoli florets and Parmesan cheese and stir lightly until just combined. Transfer to the loaf tin and bake in the oven for 40 minutes. Leave to cool in the tin for 5 minutes, then turn out on to a wire rack to cool. Serve warm or cold.

Makes 1 loaf

caramelised onion & rosemary bread

see variations page 132

Serve with a creamy vegetable soup for a delicious lunch.

for the onions
2 tbsp extra virgin olive oil
1 large onion, finely
    chopped
2 tsp dried rosemary
pinch of salt
pinch of sugar

for the bread
1 tsp sugar
320 ml (11 fl oz) warm water
2 tsp active dry yeast
510 g (1 lb 2 oz) white
    bread flour
1 tsp salt

1 tbsp olive oil + extra
    for greasing
1 bunch spring onions, finely
    chopped (green part only)

Line a large baking sheet with baking paper. First, caramelise the onions. In a large frying pan, heat the olive oil over a medium heat. Add the onions and sauté for 5 minutes until softened. Reduce heat slightly and continue to cook, stirring occasionally, until the onions are a deep golden brown. This will take approximately 25–35 minutes. Keep an eye on the frying pan. If the onions start sticking to the pan, add a little water or stock, and stir. Add a pinch of salt and a pinch of sugar to help the onions caramelise. Set aside to cool.

Dissolve the sugar in the warm water and sprinkle the yeast on top. Set aside for 10–15 minutes, until frothy. In a large bowl, mix the flour with the salt and the rosemary. Make a well in the centre, and add the yeast liquid and the olive oil. Mix well to form a soft dough. If the dough feels too dry, add more water, and if it feels too wet, add a little more flour. Add the onions and spring onions, and knead for about 10 minutes, until the dough is soft, smooth and elastic.

Put the dough into a greased bowl and turn the dough around so that it is coated all over. Cover with cling film and leave in a warm place until the dough has doubled in size, about an hour. Turn out on to a lightly floured work surface and punch down slightly. Mould into a round, slightly oval shape, and place on the lined baking sheet. Cover and leave until doubled in size, about an hour. Preheat the oven to 220°C (425°F). Dust the top of the loaf with flour and make four deep diagonal slashes in the top. Bake for about 30 minutes, or until the bottom of the bread sounds hollow when tapped. Cool on a wire rack.

Makes 1 loaf

walnut & raisin bread

see variations page 133

This walnut and raisin bread is flavoured with walnut oil and is a delicious accompaniment to creamy cheese or a sharp cheddar.

160 g (5¾ oz) white bread flour
130 g (4½ oz) wholewheat bread flour
2 tsp instant dry yeast
2 tsp brown sugar
1 tsp salt

180 ml (6 fl oz) + 2 tbsp hand-hot water
2 tsp walnut oil
85 g (3 oz) coarsely chopped walnuts
85 g (3 oz) raisins
oil for greasing

Lightly grease a large baking sheet with a little oil. In a large bowl, mix together the flours, yeast, sugar and salt, adding the yeast on one side and the salt on the other. Make a well in the centre, and add the hand-hot water and the walnut oil. Stir together until a firm dough forms. If it fails to come together properly, add a little more water, and if it feels too wet, add a little more flour. Turn out on to a lightly floured work surface, and knead for 10 minutes, until the dough is soft, smooth and elastic.

Press the dough out into a 20 x 20-cm (8 x 8-in) square, sprinkle the walnut pieces and raisins on top and roll up like a Swiss roll. Knead for 2–3 minutes to evenly distribute the fruit and nuts through the bread. Form the dough into a round loaf and cut a deep cross in the top of the loaf. Place on the baking sheet, then place inside a greased plastic bag, and leave in a warm place for an hour or so, until doubled in size. Preheat the oven to 200°C (400°F). Remove the bag and bake the bread for 35 minutes, or until it sounds hollow when tapped on the bottom. Cool on a wire rack.

Makes 1 loaf

olive & red pepper loaf

see variations page 134

A wonderful aroma will fill your kitchen while this bread is baking, and you will think of summer and the warm blue Mediterranean.

1 tbsp fine polenta	300 ml (10 fl oz) warm water
450 g (1 lb) white bread flour	3 tbsp olive oil + extra for greasing
2 tsp active dry yeast	85 g (3 oz) chopped pitted black olives
1 tsp sugar	60 g (2 oz) chopped red peppers
1 tsp salt	15 g (1/2 oz) freshly chopped basil leaves

Line a large baking sheet with baking paper and sprinkle it with 1 tablespoon fine polenta. In a large bowl, mix the flour, yeast, sugar and salt together, adding the yeast on one side and the salt on the other. Make a well in the centre and add the warm water and olive oil. Mix together to form a soft dough. Turn out on to a lightly floured work surface and knead for 10 minutes until soft, smooth and elastic. Put the dough in a large lightly oiled bowl and turn to coat it all over. Cover and put in a warm place until doubled in size, about an hour.

Turn out on to a lightly floured work surface and punch down. Add the olives, peppers and basil, and knead again until they are evenly distributed through the dough. Mould into a ball, press down firmly and sprinkle the top with white flour. Mark a deep cross in the top. Place on the lined baking sheet, cover and leave for an hour in a warm place, until almost doubled in size. Preheat the oven to 220°C (425°F). Remove the cover and bake for 30 minutes, until golden brown and the bottom of the loaf sounds hollow when tapped. Cool on a wire rack.

Makes 1 loaf

raisin, date & apricot bread

see variations page 135

This loaf is full of dried fruits; slice and spread with butter for an excellent snack.

95 g (3¹/₄ oz) + 370 g (13 oz) plain
   flour, divided
1¹/₂ tbsp active dry yeast
1 tsp sugar
240 ml (8 fl oz) warm water
85 g (3 oz) butter, cold, cut into cubes
85 g (3 oz) light brown sugar
1 tsp salt
1 tsp cinnamon

¹/₂ tsp ground ginger
¹/₄ tsp ground nutmeg
225 g (8 oz) sultanas
225 g (8 oz) stoned and chopped dried dates
100 g (4 oz) chopped dried apricots
100 g (4 oz) dried currants
1 egg, room temperature, lightly beaten
2 tbsp honey for glazing
oil for greasing

Grease two 450-g (1-lb) 20 x 10-cm (8 x 4-in) loaf tins with a little oil. Put 95 g (3¹/₄ oz) flour into a large bowl, and add yeast, sugar and warm water. Mix well and leave until frothy, about 20 minutes. Put 370 g (13 oz) flour into a large bowl, add the butter and cut in until the mixture resembles fine breadcrumbs. Stir in sugar, salt, spices and dried fruit. Add the egg and flour mixture to the yeast liquid, and mix well until it forms a dough. Turn out on to a lightly floured work surface and knead for 10 minutes, until the dough is smooth and elastic. Put in a large lightly greased bowl and turn to coat it all over. Cover and put in a warm place for an hour or so, until doubled in size. Preheat the oven to 180°C (350°F). Turn the dough out on to a lightly floured work surface and punch down. Knead again for 3–4 minutes, divide in half and shape to fit the loaf tins. Cover and leave in a warm place for about 45 minutes, until the dough has risen 2.5 cm (1 in) above the tins. Bake for about an hour, until they sound hollow when tapped on the bottom. Cool on a wire rack; brush with honey while warm.

Makes 2 loaves

pecan & cranberry rye bread

see variations page 136

The rye flour and pecans in this bread add extra texture and interest.

85 g (3 oz) rye flour
280 g (10 oz) white bread flour
115 g (4 oz) whole wheat flour
1 tsp salt
4 tsp active dry yeast

2 tbsp olive oil
2 tbsp molasses
350 ml (12½ fl oz) warm water
200g (7 oz) chopped pecans
100 g (3½ oz) dried cranberries

Line a large cookie sheet with parchment paper. In the bowl of a stand mixer with a dough hook attachment, combine the 3 flours together. Add the salt on one side and the yeast on the other. Make a well in the centre and, mixing at a low speed, add the oil, molasses, and warm water. Knead at medium speed for 8 minutes. Add the pecans and cranberries, and mix for 1 minute. Transfer the dough to a large lightly greased bowl and turn to coat it all over. Cover and put in a warm place for an hour or so, until the dough has doubled in size.

Turn the dough out onto a lightly floured work surface and punch down. Flatten into a rectangle and roll up like a jellyroll, flatten again, and roll up much tighter so that it becomes an oblong shape approximately 30 cm (12 in) long. Transfer to the cookie sheet with the seam underneath, loosely cover, and leave for about an hour, until doubled in size. Preheat the oven to 200°C (400°F). Rub flour all over the top of the loaf, and make deep diagonal cuts across the top in both directions forming diamond shapes. Bake for 35 minutes, until the bottom of the loaf sounds hollow when tapped. Remove from the oven and cool on a wire rack.

Makes 1 loaf

cardamom braided loaf

see variations page 137

Cardamom is a wonderfully versatile spice. Used sparingly, it is equally at home in sweet or savoury dishes.

1 tsp + 130 g (5 oz) sugar, divided + extra
   for sprinkling
355 ml (12 fl oz) whole milk + extra for brushing
4 tsp active dry yeast
100 g (4 oz) butter + extra for greasing

2 eggs, room temperature
1 tsp salt
2 tsp ground cardamom seeds
115 g (4 oz) wholewheat flour
625 g (1 lb 6 oz) plain flour

Lightly grease two large baking sheets with butter. Dissolve 1 teaspoon sugar in 300 ml (10 fl oz) warm milk, sprinkle the yeast on top and leave for 10–15 minutes until frothy. In the bowl of a stand mixer with a paddle attachment, beat the butter and 135 g (4¾ oz) sugar together until creamy. Add the eggs, one at a time, beating each time. Add the yeast liquid, mix until combined and add the salt and ground cardamom. Gradually add the wholewheat flour and enough plain flour to make a moderately soft dough. Switch to a dough hook attachment and knead for 5–8 minutes, until the dough is smooth and elastic. Place the dough in a large oiled bowl and turn to coat it all over. Cover and put in a warm place until doubled in size, about an hour.

Turn the dough out on to a lightly floured work surface, punch down and knead again for 2 minutes. Divide the dough in half, and each half into thirds. Roll the pieces of dough into six balls and leave to rest for 10 minutes. Roll each ball into a 15-cm (6-in)-long rope, and place three ropes about 2.5 cm (1 in) apart on each baking sheet. Beginning in the middle, braid the dough loosely towards each end, pinch the ends together and tuck under the loaves.

Place one sheet somewhere warm for about 45 minutes, until almost doubled in size. Leave the other baking sheet at room temperature for 20 minutes longer; this will give you time to bake the first loaf before the other is ready.

Preheat the oven to 190°C (375°F). Remove the first loaf from the plastic bag, brush with milk, sprinkle with sugar and bake for about 20 minutes, until golden brown. The bottom of the loaf should be browned as well. Cool on a wire rack. Check that the other loaf is ready, brush with milk and sugar and bake for 20 minutes.

Makes 2 loaves

pesto & sundried tomato loaf

see variations page 138

Pesto can be used in so many ways, not least in a bread, paired with sundried tomatoes.

1 tsp sugar dissolved in	90 g (3¼ oz) wholewheat flour	3 tbsp finely chopped
395 ml (13 fl oz) warm water	½ tsp salt	sundried tomatoes
4 tsp active dry yeast	2 tbsp olive oil	(well drained if in oil)
415 g (15 oz) white bread flour	4 tbsp pesto (see page 138)	2 tsp red chilli flakes

Line a large baking sheet with baking paper. Sprinkle the yeast on to the sugar–water mix and leave for 10–15 minutes until frothy. In the bowl of a stand mixer with a dough hook attachment, combine the flours and salt. Make a well in the centre, add the yeast liquid and olive oil and mix until a soft dough forms. Knead for 5–8 minutes until the dough is soft, smooth and elastic. Transfer to a large, lightly oiled bowl and turn to coat it all over. Cover and put in a warm place for an hour or so, until doubled in size. Turn the dough out on to a lightly floured work surface, divide into four equal pieces, roll each into a ball and leave to rest for 10 minutes. Roll each ball into a 15-cm (6-in)-long rope, and place about 2.5 cm (1 in) apart on the baking sheet. Cut a deep groove into each rope, and spoon a little pesto and some chopped sundried tomatoes along each groove. Bring the dough up over the pesto and tomatoes, sealing the mixture inside and hiding it. Beginning in the middle, braid the dough loosely towards each end and tuck the ends together, forming a rough circle. Put in a warm place for about 45 minutes, until almost doubled in size. Preheat the oven to 220°C (425°F). Brush the loaf with a little olive oil, sprinkle with crushed red chilli flakes, and bake for 10 minutes. Reduce the oven temperature to 170°C (325°F) and bake for another 15 minutes, until golden brown. Remove from the oven and cool on a wire rack. Serve warm.

Makes 1 loaf

cheese & celery loaf

see variations page 139

Cheese and celery are a classic combination, and this bread is excellent to use for ham sandwiches.

450 g (1 lb) self-raising flour
1 tsp salt
30 g (1 oz) cold, cut into cubes
3 large sticks celery, washed and finely chopped
1 clove garlic, finely crushed

150g (5½ oz) finely shredded cheddar cheese
2 tsp dried chives
1 egg, room temperature
200 ml (7 fl oz) whole milk
2 tsp Dijon mustard
oil for greasing

Preheat the oven to 220°C (425°F) and lightly grease a 450-g (1-lb) 20 x 10-cm (8 x 4-in) loaf tin with a little oil. In a large bowl, sieve the flour and salt together. Cut in the butter until the mixture resembles fine breadcrumbs. Add celery, garlic, cheese and dried chives, and stir lightly to combine. Whisk the egg, milk and mustard together, and add gradually to the flour mixture, mixing to form a soft dough. Knead lightly and quickly on a lightly floured work surface, and shape into an oblong to fit the loaf tin. Bake for 55 minutes, or until golden brown. Remove from the oven and cool on a wire rack.

Makes 1 loaf

variations

banana & cranberry loaf

see base recipe page 113

toasted banana & cranberry loaf with caramelised apples
Prepare the basic recipe, cut into slices and toast. Peel, core and slice four apples. Melt
4 tablespoons unsalted butter over medium-high heat. Once the butter has almost melted,
add 6 tablespoons brown sugar, 1 teaspoon cinnamon and the apples. Cook and toss the
apples a few times until they are nicely caramelised on all sides. Spread the toast slices
with chocolate hazelnut spread and top with apples.

dark chocolate & raspberry banana bread
Prepare the basic recipe, replacing the cranberries with fresh raspberries and adding
1 teaspoon vanilla extract and 200 g (7 oz) dark chocolate chunks or chips with the
last banana.

banana & pineapple loaf
Prepare the basic recipe, replacing the cranberries with candied or freeze-dried pineapple.
Add 25 g (¾ oz) flaked coconut and 1 teaspoon coconut extract with the last banana.

dairy-free brazil nut & chocolate banana bread
Prepare the basic recipe, replacing the buttermilk and butter with full-fat coconut milk and
sunflower oil. Replace the cranberries with 60 g (2 oz) chopped brazil nuts and 150 g (6 oz)
dark chocolate chunks or chips.

variations

broccoli bread

see base recipe page 115

asparagus bread
Prepare the basic recipe, replacing the broccoli with 100 g (4 oz) cooked chopped asparagus.

pepper bread
Prepare the basic recipe, replacing the broccoli with 100 g (4 oz) roasted, skinned and seeded red and green peppers.

courgette bread
Prepare the basic recipe, replacing the broccoli with chopped sautéed courgette. Cut 1 large courgette into slices and cut each slice in half. Melt 1 tablespoon olive oil in a large frying pan and, over a medium-high heat, sauté the courgette for a few minutes until tender. Cool.

aubergine bread
Prepare the basic recipe, replacing the broccoli with chopped oven-roasted aubergine. Chop 1 medium aubergine, place it on a large baking sheet, drizzle with oil and season with salt, freshly ground black pepper and 1 teaspoon mixed herbs. Roast at 190°C (375°F) for 25 minutes. Cool.

variations

caramelised onion & rosemary bread

see base recipe page 116

caramelised onion & basil bread
Prepare the basic recipe, replacing the rosemary with 15 g (1/2 oz) chopped basil.

caramelised onion, cheese & tomato bread
Prepare the basic recipe. Add 60 g (2 oz) grated cheddar cheese and 40 g (1 1/2 oz) chopped sundried tomatoes with the onions.

caramelised onion, bacon & parsley bread
Prepare the basic recipe, omitting the rosemary and adding 15 g (1/2 oz) chopped parsley and 5 slices of bacon, cooked until crispy and crumbled, with the onions.

caramelised onion, goat's cheese, coriander & olive bread
Prepare the basic recipe. Omit the rosemary and add 40 g (1 1/2 oz) chopped goat's cheese, 40 g (1 1/2 oz) pitted and chopped black olives, and 15 g (1/2 oz) chopped coriander with the onions.

walnut & raisin bread

see base recipe page 119

walnut, date & fig bread
Prepare the basic recipe, replacing the raisins with 125 g (4½ oz) chopped, dried ready-to-eat dates and 4 chopped dried figs.

walnut, prune & blueberry bread
Prepare the basic recipe, replacing the raisins with 60 g (2 oz) chopped pitted prunes and 60 g (2 oz) fresh blueberries.

pecan & peach bread
Prepare the basic recipe, replacing the chopped walnuts and raisins with 40 g (1½ oz) chopped pecans and 1 stoned, chopped peach.

coffee & walnut bread
Prepare the basic recipe, adding 2 teaspoons instant coffee powder, dissolved in the hand-hot water.

variations

olive & red pepper loaf

see base recipe page 120

olive, courgette & red pepper loaf
Prepare the basic recipe, adding ½ a courgette, chopped and sautéed in a little olive oil and cooled, with the olives.

olive, aubergine & red pepper loaf
Prepare the basic recipe, adding ½ small aubergine, chopped, oven-roasted and cooled, with the olives.

olive, tomato, pepper & bacon loaf
Prepare the basic recipe, adding 40 g (1½ oz) chopped sundried tomatoes and 4 slices of bacon, cooked until crispy and crumbled, with the olives.

olive, cheese, pepper & tomato loaf
Prepare the basic recipe, adding 60 g (2 oz) grated cheddar cheese and 40 g (1½ oz) chopped sundried tomatoes with the olives.

variations

raisin, date & apricot bread

see base recipe page 122

orange, cardamom & almond bread
Prepare the original recipe, replacing the dates with 85 g (3 oz) chopped almonds. Add 1 teaspoon crushed cardamom seeds and the zest of 1 orange with the dried fruit.

raisin, poppy seed & apricot bread
Prepare the basic recipe, replacing 125 g (4½ oz) of the currants with 125 g (4½ oz) poppy seeds.

dairy-free cherry & pecan bread
Prepare the basic recipe, replacing the butter with sunflower oil, the sultanas with dried cherries and the dates with chopped pecans.

raisin, fig & walnut bread
Prepare the basic recipe, replacing the currants with chopped dried figs and the apricots with chopped walnuts.

pecan & cranberry rye bread

see base recipe page 123

pecan & tropical fruit rye bread
Prepare the basic recipe, replacing the cranberries with chopped candied or freeze-dried tropical fruit.

pecan, cranberry & mango rye bread
Prepare the basic recipe, adding 55 g (2 oz) freshly chopped mango.

pecan, pear & dark chocolate rye bread
Prepare the basic recipe, replacing the cranberries with 2 peeled, cored, chopped pears and adding 100 g (3½ oz) dark chocolate chips.

pecan, cranberry & plum rye bread
Prepare the basic recipe, adding 3 stoned, chopped ripe plums.

variations

cardamom braided loaf

see base recipe page 124

sultana & ginger braided loaf
Prepare the basic recipe, replacing the cardamom with 2 teaspoons ground ginger and adding 170 g (6 oz) sultanas with the wholewheat flour.

apple & cinnamon braided loaf
Prepare the basic recipe, replacing the cardamom with 2 teaspoons cinnamon and adding 170 g (6 oz) chopped dried apples with the wholewheat flour.

chocolate & hazelnut braided loaf
Prepare the basic recipe, replacing the cardamom with 2 teaspoons vanilla extract, added with the yeast liquid, and adding 150 g (5½ oz) chocolate chips and 40 g (1½ oz) toasted and chopped hazelnuts with the wholewheat flour.

raisin & nutmeg braided loaf
Prepare the basic recipe, replacing the cardamom with 1 teaspoon ground nutmeg and adding 170 g (6 oz) raisins with the wholewheat flour.

variations

pesto & sundried tomato loaf

see base recipe page 127

homemade pesto
Put 60 g (2 oz) basil leaves into a food processor and pulse to a pulp. Add 1 small clove of garlic and 60 g (2 oz) toasted pine nuts, and blend until mixed through. Stir in 120 ml (4 fl oz) extra virgin olive oil and 30 g (1 oz) grated Parmesan. This will keep for up to 2 weeks in a sterile jar in the fridge.

pesto, sundried tomato & bacon loaf
Prepare the basic recipe. Add 4 slices of bacon, cooked until crispy and crumbled, to the sundried tomato pieces in the grooves.

pesto swirl loaf
Prepare the basic recipe. After first rising, turn the dough out on to a lightly floured work surface and divide in half. Punch down and press each half into a rectangle about 20 x 20 cm (8 x 8 in). Spread pesto on dough and roll up like a Swiss roll. Place in two 450-g (1-lb) loaf tins and set to rise again. Bake in preheated oven at 180°C (350°F) for 30–35 minutes.

pesto & sundried tomato loaf with parmesan
Prepare the basic recipe, adding 30 g (1 oz) grated Parmesan cheese to the sundried tomatoes in the grooves.

variations

cheese & celery loaf

see base recipe page 129

cheese & corn bread
Prepare the basic recipe, replacing the celery with 450 g (1 lb) whole-kernel corn.

cheese & olive topper
Prepare the basic recipe. Cut the loaf into slices. Roughly chop one small tin black olives, one small jar pimento-stuffed green olives and 2 thinly sliced spring onions, and add to a bowl with 50 g (2 oz) butter, 100 g (4 oz) mayonnaise, and 340 g (12 oz) grated Monterey Jack cheese. Spread on the slices of bread and bake in the oven at 170°C (325°F) for 20 minutes, or until the cheese has melted and browned.

cheese & bacon loaf
Prepare the basic recipe, adding 4 slices of bacon, cooked until crispy and crumbled, with the egg.

cheese & tomato loaf
Prepare the basic recipe, adding 2 tomatoes, skinned, seeded and chopped, with the egg.

flatbreads
& pizzas

From Middle Eastern flatbread to stuffed-crust

pizza, in this chapter you will find inspiration

for traditional favourites with wonderful flavours.

Swap the toppings and bases of the pizzas around

to suit your personal preference.

garlic & coriander naan bread

see variations page 161

These naan taste authentic and make a great accompaniment to an Indian curry.

2 tsp sugar, divided
160 ml (5 fl oz) warm milk
2 tsp active dry yeast
450 g (1 lb) plain flour
$\frac{1}{2}$ tsp salt

1 tsp baking powder
2 tbsp olive oil
160 ml (5 fl oz) natural yoghurt
1 egg, room temperature, lightly beaten
3 tbsp freshly chopped coriander

Dissolve 1 teaspoon sugar in the warm milk, sprinkle the yeast on top and leave for 10–15 minutes until frothy. In a large bowl, sieve the flour, salt and baking powder. Add the remaining teaspoon of sugar, yeast liquid and the remaining ingredients, and mix until it forms a soft dough. Knead for 10 minutes until the dough is soft, smooth and elastic. Transfer to a large lightly oiled bowl and turn to coat it all over. Cover and put in a warm place for an hour or so, until doubled in size. Preheat your oven to the highest temperature, and place a heavy roasting tin into it. Preheat the grill. Turn the dough out on to a lightly floured work surface, punch down and knead again for 2–3 minutes. Divide the dough into six equal pieces, and roll each one into a ball. Keep five covered. Roll the sixth into a tear-shaped naan, about 25 cm (10 in) long and about 12. 5 cm (5 in) at the widest point. Remove the roasting tin from the oven, and slap the naan down on to it. Quickly put it back and bake for 3 minutes. It should puff up. Remove the roasting tin from the oven and immediately place it under the grill, about 7.5–10 cm (3–4 in) away from the heat, for about 30 seconds only, or until the top of the naan begins to brown. Wrap the naan in a clean kitchen towel and keep warm. Repeat with the rest of the naan. Serve hot.

Makes 6 naan

tortillas

see variations page 162

If you don't have a tortilla press, simply roll these with a rolling pin. Just get them nice and thin, and the result will be perfect.

255 g (9 oz) plain flour
1¹/₂ tsp baking powder
1 tsp salt

1 tbsp sunflower oil + extra for greasing
180 ml (6 fl oz) warm whole milk

In the bowl of a stand mixer with a paddle attachment, on a low speed, mix together the flour, baking powder and salt. Slowly add the oil and warm milk, and mix until a dough forms. Mix for 3–4 minutes, until the dough is soft and supple. Transfer the dough to a large lightly oiled bowl, cover and leave to rest for 20 minutes. Turn the dough out on to a lightly floured work surface, and divide into eight pieces. Form each piece into a ball, cover and leave to rest for 10 minutes.

On a lightly oiled work surface, roll out each ball of dough into a thin circle. Either press in a tortilla press or use a rolling pin to roll it as thin as you can. Over a high heat, heat a large frying pan, and when it is really hot, drop a tortilla in and cook for 30 seconds on each side. It will puff up and form bubbles. Press down on the tortilla with a spatula while it is cooking, so that it browns all over. Remove from the frying pan, cover and keep warm while you cook all the tortillas.

Makes 8 tortillas

pitta bread

see variations page 163

Pittas are best eaten immediately, and freeze well, but you can store them in an airtight container for 1–2 days, and reheat in the toaster.

2 tsp sugar, divided
240 ml (8 fl oz) warm water
2 tsp active dry yeast
320 g (11 oz) plain flour

2 tsp salt
2 tsp olive oil + extra for greasing
fine polenta

Dissolve 1 teaspoon sugar in the warm water, sprinkle the yeast on top and leave for 10–15 minutes until frothy. In a large bowl, sieve the flour and salt together, and add the remaining teaspoon of sugar. Make a well in the centre, add the yeast liquid and olive oil, and mix until a dough forms. Turn the dough out on to a lightly oiled work surface and knead for 10 minutes, until the dough is soft, silky and elastic. Transfer to a large lightly oiled bowl and turn to coat it all over. Cover and put in a warm place for an hour, until doubled in size.

Preheat the oven to 220°C (425°F) and put a large roasting tin on the middle shelf. Turn the dough out on to a work surface sprinkled with fine polenta. Knead the dough for 2 minutes until all the air is knocked out and it is smooth. Divide into eight, and form each piece into a ball. With a rolling pin, roll each into an oval shape, about 3 mm ($\frac{1}{8}$ in) thick. If your roasting tin has enough space for four pittas with a little space in between, prepare four and keep the rest covered. Remove the roasting tin from the oven, quickly sprinkle with fine polenta and arrange the pitta breads, leaving a little space in between. Bake for 5–8 minutes; they should puff up. Remove the pittas when they have ballooned. Repeat with the remaining dough.

Makes 8 pittas

carly's middle-eastern flatbread

see variations page 164

This recipe is wheat- and gluten-free, dairy-free, yeast-free and absolutely delicious, especially with hummus. Eat it the day you make it, as it does not keep well.

130 g (4^1/$_2$ oz) rice flour
85 g (3 oz) tapioca flour
40 g (1^1/$_2$ oz) potato starch
^{1}/$_2$ tsp xanthan gum
^{1}/$_2$ tsp bicarbonate of soda
^{1}/$_2$ tsp salt

2 tsp cumin seeds
50 ml (2 fl oz) orange juice
50 ml (2 fl oz) extra virgin olive oil + 6 tbsp
    for frying
50 ml (2 fl oz) rice milk
water as needed

In a large bowl, combine all the ingredients. Add 1 tablespoon of water at a time until the dough holds together. Turn the dough out on to a floured surface and break into quarters. Mould each quarter into a ball and roll into an oval 1.5 cm (^{1}/$_2$ in) thick. The dough will break easily and the edges will be rough, so just pinch them a bit with your fingers.

In a large frying pan, add 6 tablespoons extra virgin olive oil and heat for 5 minutes. When the oil is hot, but not smoking, add two of the flatbreads and fry for 3 minutes each side. Continue with the remaining flatbreads. Serve hot or warm.

Makes 4 flatbreads

rosemary & olive oil flatbread

see variations page 165

This flatbread recipe is made using pizza dough, and is great grilled on the barbecue, but equally delicious cooked over a high heat in a frying pan on the hob.

1 portion pizza dough (see salami pizza recipe page 149)
extra virgin olive oil for brushing

a few rosemary sprigs, leaves only
coarse sea salt

Prepare the basic pizza dough recipe. Punch down and divide into eight pieces. Roll each piece into an oval shape about 6 mm ($1/4$ in) thick.

Heat a large frying pan over a medium-high heat, brush with olive oil and cook each flatbread for 3–4 minutes each side, until golden brown and slightly charred. Mix a little olive oil with the rosemary leaves and brush over the flatbreads, sprinkle with salt and serve immediately.

Makes 8 flatbreads

salami, tomato & basil pizza

see variations page 166

Making your own pizza is not only easy, but fun, healthy and cheap!

1 tsp sugar dissolved in
    355 ml (12 fl oz) warm water
2 tsp active dry yeast
510 g (1 lb 2 oz) white bread flour
2 tsp salt

10 tbsp pizza sauce
    (see sourdough crust
    recipe page 150)
20 fresh basil leaves
8 slices salami

200 g (8 oz) mozzarella
    cheese, sliced
olive oil for greasing and
    drizzling
fine polenta

Sprinkle the yeast on top of the sugar–water mix, and leave for 10–15 minutes until frothy. In a large bowl, mix the flour and salt together. Make a well in the centre, pour in the yeast liquid and mix together until a soft dough forms. Turn the dough out on to a lightly floured work surface, and knead for 10 minutes until the dough is soft, smooth and elastic. Dust the top of the dough with flour, cover with cling film, and leave to rest for 15–20 minutes at room temperature. This makes it easier to roll the dough. Divide the dough in half. It is best to roll the dough out 15–20 minutes before baking it.

Preheat the oven to 260°C (500°F), and put a large roasting tin or pizza stone on the middle shelf. Dust your work surface with a little fine polenta, take each piece of dough and roll out to circles about 6 mm (¼ in) thick. Cut two pieces of aluminium foil slightly bigger than the pizza bases, brush them with a little olive oil, dust with fine polenta and place the bases on top. Spread each base evenly with 5 tablespoons pizza sauce, add the basil leaves, lay the salami on top and place small slices of mozzarella in the gaps. Bake one at a time in the middle of a very hot oven for 8–10 minutes only, until golden and crisp. Serve immediately.

Makes 2 large pizzas

sourdough crust with sausage, pepper & mushrooms

see variations page 167

Sourdough makes a great pizza crust. Use the pizza sauce in this recipe for all the pizzas in this chapter, and it is also good with pasta or fish.

for pizza sauce
1 tbsp olive oil
1 large onion, finely chopped
2 cloves garlic, crushed
two 400 g (14 oz) tins chopped tomatoes
1 vegetable or chicken stock cube
1 tbsp Worcestershire sauce
1 tsp sugar
8 tbsp tomato purée
1 tsp dried oregano
8 basil leaves, torn

for the topping
10 tbsp pizza sauce (see recipe below)
340 g (12 oz) Italian sausage, cooked, crumbled
    and drained
300 g (10 oz) sliced mushrooms, lightly sautéed,
    and drained
1 bell pepper, seeds removed, sliced thinly
450 g (1 lb) grated Provolone cheese

$^1/_2$ quantity sourdough (see recipe page 34)
fine polenta, for dusting

Make the pizza sauce. (This recipe makes more than you need, but it is so versatile, I like to keep some in the fridge or freezer.) In a medium saucepan over a medium heat, add the oil, and sauté the onion and garlic for about 5 minutes, until softened. Add chopped tomatoes with juice, stock cube, Worcestershire sauce, sugar, tomato purée, dried herbs and torn basil leaves, and simmer until thickened. Season to taste with salt and freshly ground black pepper. Set aside to cool, and chill in the fridge.

Heat oven to 230°C (450°F). Divide the sourdough in half, and roll each piece into a circle about 6 mm (¼ in) thick. Cut two pieces of aluminium foil slightly bigger than the pizza bases, brush them with a little olive oil, dust with fine polenta and place the bases on top. Spread each pizza base evenly with 5 tablespoons pizza sauce and a quarter of the cheese, then sprinkle on half the crumbled sausage, half of the mushrooms, half of the pepper, and the remaining quarter of cheese. Bake directly on the oven shelf for 10 minutes, or until the base is crisp and the cheese has melted. Serve immediately.

Makes 2 medium pizzas

express stuffed-crust pepperoni pizza

see variations page 168

This is a quick pizza dough to mix together and, if available, string cheese is the secret to the stuffed crust. Children especially will love extra pizza sauce for dipping.

255 g (9 oz) white bread flour
1 tsp sugar
1 tsp instant dry yeast
1 tsp salt
180 ml (6 fl oz) warm water
1 tsp olive oil

7 mozzarella cheese sticks or 175 g (6 oz) finely grated mozzarella
8 tbsp pizza sauce
120 g (4 oz) grated cheddar cheese

60 g (2 oz) sliced mushrooms, lightly sautéed, drained
24 slices pepperoni
120 g (4 oz) grated mozzarella cheese
2 tbsp cornmeal for sprinkling

Sprinkle a large pizza stone or baking sheet with fine polenta. In the bowl of a stand mixer fitted with a dough hook attachment, add the flour and sugar. Add the yeast on one side and the salt on the other. Make a well in the centre and add the warm water and olive oil. Mix until a dough begins to form. Knead on a slow speed for 5 minutes. Roll out the pizza dough to a circle about 35 cm (14 in) in diameter and transfer it to the baking sheet. Sprinkle with fine polenta and cover with cling film. Leave at room temperature for 30 minutes. Preheat the oven to 230°C (450°F). Cut the mozzarella sticks into 2.5-cm (1-in) lengths, and arrange around the outside of the pizza crust, about 2.5 cm (1 in) from the edge. Or place the grated mozzarella around the outside. Bring the edge of the dough up and over the cheese to form the stuffed rim, and pinch it to seal it well. Spread the pizza crust with pizza sauce, cheddar, mushrooms, pepperoni and mozzarella. Bake for 15–20 minutes, until the crust is golden brown and the cheese has melted. Serve immediately.

Makes 1 large pizza

yeast-free chilli seafood pizza

see variations page 169

This pizza is loaded with crabmeat, shrimp and mozzarella, and with garlic and tomatoes, it is a pizza fit for a king.

for the topping
4 cloves garlic, crushed
2 tbsp extra virgin olive oil
1 small tin crabmeat
175 g (6 oz) peeled, cooked
   shrimp
1 tbsp fresh parsley, chopped

5 tbsp pizza sauce (see recipe
   page 150)
175 g (6 oz) grated mozzarella
   cheese, divided
30 g (1 oz) grated Romano
   cheese
1 small red chilli, seeded and
   finely chopped

for the crust
190 g (6¾ oz) plain flour
1 tbsp baking powder
½ tsp salt
1 tsp Italian mixed herbs
120 ml (4 fl oz) water
2 tbsp extra virgin olive oil

In a large frying pan over a medium-low heat, sauté the garlic in the olive oil for 5 minutes, remove from the heat and set aside to cool. Transfer to a medium bowl and add the crabmeat, shrimp and parsley, mixing well with the olive oil and garlic. Set aside.

Preheat the oven to 200°C (400°F). Make the crust. In a large bowl, sieve the flour, baking powder and salt together. Stir in the herbs. Make a well in the centre, and add 120 ml (4 fl oz) water and 2 tablespoons olive oil. Mix together by gradually incorporating the flour into the liquid, until a dough comes together. Turn out on to a lightly floured work surface and knead gently for 5 minutes, until the dough is smooth and elastic. Roll out into a circle about 25 cm (10 in) in diameter. Transfer to a baking sheet. Spread the pizza crust with the pizza sauce, add the crabmeat and shrimp mixture, sprinkle with chilli and top with the cheeses. Bake for 15–20 minutes, until the crust is golden brown, and the cheese has melted. Serve immediately.

Makes 1 medium pizza

gluten-free spinach, basil & mozzarella pizza

see variations page 170

When cooking gluten-free, be careful that you do not cross-contaminate with products containing or in contact with gluten, including utensils, work surfaces and baking tins.

for the crust
175 g (6 oz) rice flour
115 g (3$\frac{1}{2}$ oz) tapioca flour
85 g (3 oz) potato starch
2 tsp xanthan gum
1 tsp sugar
1 tsp agar agar or unflavoured
   gelatin powder
1 tsp sugar

1 tsp salt
2 tsp instant dry yeast
355 ml (12 fl oz) warm water
1 tbsp extra virgin olive oil
1$\frac{1}{2}$ tsp rice wine vinegar

for the topping
60 g (2 oz) fresh baby spinach
   leaves

salt and freshly ground
   black pepper to taste
8 tbsp pizza sauce (see recipe
   page 150)
240 g (9 oz) mozzarella
   cheese
30 g ($\frac{3}{4}$ oz) fresh basil leaves
2 tbsp fine polenta

Line two large baking sheets with baking paper and sprinkle with polenta. In the bowl of a stand mixer with a dough hook attachment, mix all the dry ingredients for the crust together, adding the salt on one side and the yeast on the other. Make a well in the centre, and add the warm water, olive oil and rice vinegar. Mix until a dough forms. Knead on a low speed for 5 minutes, and turn out onto a work surface dusted with fine polenta.

Divide the dough in half. Sprinkle polenta over half of the dough, and roll it out to about a 30-cm (12-in) circle. Transfer it to a baking sheet, dust with polenta, cover with cling film and put in a warm place for 1 hour. Repeat this process with the other half of the dough.

Preheat the oven to 200°C (400°F). Bake the pizza crusts for 5 minutes, and remove from the oven. In a large frying pan, heat 2 teaspoons olive oil, and fry the spinach in batches for a few seconds until just wilted. Remove from the heat and season with a little salt and freshly ground black pepper. Spread 4 tablespoons pizza sauce on each pizza crust. Break off pieces of mozzarella and lay them on the pizzas. Scatter with the wilted spinach leaves and the basil leaves, and bake for 10–12 minutes. Serve immediately.

Makes 2 large pizzas

polenta pan pizza with oven-roasted mediterranean vegetables

see variations page 171

Spicy instant polenta is cooked in a large frying pan, covered with delicious oven-roasted Mediterranean vegetables.

4 ripe tomatoes
1 large aubergine, cut into large chunks
2 red peppers, seeded and cut into chunks

1 red onion, cut into wedges
2 cloves garlic, finely chopped
2 tbsp fresh rosemary leaves
salt and freshly ground black pepper to taste

3 tbsp extra virgin olive oil
240 g (8 oz) quick-cooking polenta
3 tbsp freshly grated Parmesan cheese

Preheat the oven to 230°C (450°F). Put the vegetables in a large roasting tin, sprinkle the garlic and rosemary leaves on top and season with salt and freshly ground black pepper. Drizzle with olive oil, toss together and roast for 40 minutes.

While the vegetables are roasting, cook the polenta according to the package instructions. Pour it into a medium-size frying pan and leave to set for about 10 minutes. Sprinkle with Parmesan cheese and place under the grill for 3–4 minutes, until golden and bubbling. Top with the roasted vegetables and serve immediately.

Makes 1 medium pan pizza

parmesan & garlic breadsticks

see variations page 172

Large, soft, chewy and flavoured with Parmesan and garlic, this is the best recipe for breadsticks ever.

1 tsp + 1^1/$_2$ tbsp sugar, divided
355 ml (12 fl oz) warm water
2 tsp active dry yeast
450 g (1 lb) white bread flour
1 tsp salt
2 tbsp olive oil

to finish
100 g (4 oz) butter
1 tbsp garlic salt, divided
40 g (1^1/$_2$ oz) finely grated Parmesan
    cheese, divided
1 tbsp freshly chopped parsley, divided

Dissolve 1 teaspoon sugar in the warm water, sprinkle the yeast on top and leave for 10–15 minutes until frothy. In the bowl of a stand mixer with a dough hook attachment, combine the flour, 1^1/$_2$ tablespoons sugar and salt. Make a well in the centre, pour in the yeast liquid and add the olive oil. Mix until a soft dough forms. Knead for 5 minutes. Transfer to a large lightly oiled bowl and turn to coat it all over. Cover and put in a warm place for an hour or so, until doubled in size. Preheat the oven to 200°C (400°F). In a small tin over gentle heat, melt the butter and pour on to a large Swiss roll tin. Sprinkle the butter with garlic salt and Parmesan cheese. Turn the dough out on to a lightly floured work surface, punch down and knead for 1–2 minutes. Roll the dough out to a rectangle 30 x 40 cm (12 x 16 in), and cut into 12 x 2.5-cm (1-in) strips. Double the long strips of dough in half, and twist to form breadsticks. Roll each breadstick in the butter in the tin until completely covered. When all the breadsticks are in the tin, sprinkle with a little more garlic salt, Parmesan cheese and parsley. Bake for 12–15 minutes, until golden brown. Cool on a wire rack, and serve warm.

Makes 12 breadsticks

sundried tomato & olive sticks

see variations page 173

This dough is quite wet, so do not be tempted to add more flour during mixing.

510 g (1 lb 2 oz) white bread flour
1 tsp dried rosemary
2 tsp salt
2 tsp instant dry yeast
395 ml (13 fl oz) warm water

3 tbsp extra virgin olive oil + extra for greasing
100 g (4 oz) pitted and chopped black olives
100 g (4 oz) chopped sundried tomatoes (well
    drained if in oil)
fine polenta, to dust

Grease a large, deep rectangular baking dish with a little oil, and line two or three large baking sheets with baking paper. In the bowl of a stand mixer fitted with a dough hook attachment, combine the flour and dried rosemary. Add the salt on one side of the bowl, and the yeast on the other. Add the warm water, and on a slow speed, mix until the dough starts to come together. Knead at a slow speed for 5–8 minutes, until the dough is smooth and stretches easily (see stretch test, page 12). Add the olive oil and continue to knead for another 2 minutes. Add the olives and sundried tomatoes, and mix until just combined. Transfer to the baking dish, cover and put in a warm place for an hour or so, until doubled in size. Sprinkle your work surface with fine polenta. Carefully turn the dough out on to the work surface. Try not to knock out the air; it will still be quite wet. Dust the top of the dough with flour and fine polenta. Pull the dough out gently to a rough rectangle, and starting at one of the long sides, cut the dough into about 16 strips. Stretch each piece until it measures about 23 cm (9 in) in length. Arrange on the baking sheets about 2.5 cm (1 in) apart. Put each baking sheet inside a greased plastic bag, in a warm place for 30 minutes. Preheat the oven to 220°C (425°F). Remove the plastic bags and bake for 10–12 minutes. Cool on a wire rack.

Makes 16 breadsticks

garlic & coriander naan bread

see base recipe page 141

onion, garlic & coriander naan bread
Prepare the basic recipe, adding 30 g (1 oz) onions to the flour.

tomato, garlic & coriander naan bread
Prepare the basic recipe, adding 30 g (1 oz) skinned, seeded, chopped tomatoes to the flour.

stuffed garlic & coriander naan bread
Prepare the basic recipe. Cook 2 diced medium potatoes with 1 small finely chopped onion, 2 tablespoons chopped coriander, ½ teaspoon turmeric, ½ teaspoon garam masala and salt and pepper to taste, in 1 tablespoon oil over a very gentle heat, until tender. Take 1 ball of dough, press it down and place a small amount of potato on it. Enclose by bringing the dough up around it. Roll out to a circle and cook as directed.

garlic & coriander naan with coconut dhal
Prepare the basic recipe and serve with dhal. In a large pan, boil 300 ml (10 fl oz) water, and simmer 255 g (9 oz) red lentils with one 400 g (14 oz) tin coconut milk, 1 finely chopped onion, 2 chopped tomatoes, 2 chopped green chillies and 1 teaspoon turmeric for 20 minutes, until tender. Garnish with chopped coriander.

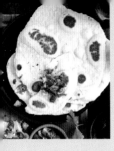

variations

tortillas

see base recipe page 142

basil, oregano & rosemary tortillas
Prepare the basic recipe, adding 1 teaspoon each of dried basil, oregano and rosemary to the flour.

fajita-seasoned tortillas
Prepare the basic recipe, adding 2 teaspoons of fajita seasoning to the flour. For fajita seasoning, mix together 4 teaspoons chilli powder, 2 teaspoons dried oregano, 2 teaspoons ground cumin and 2 teaspoons garlic salt.

tortilla shells for salad
Prepare the basic recipe. Brush both sides of each tortilla with olive oil, and season with salt and black pepper. Press each tortilla onto an upside-down ovenproof bowl, and bake in a preheated oven at 180°C (350°F) for about 15 minutes. Cool on a wire rack and fill with salad.

coriander & chilli tortillas
Prepare the basic recipe, adding 1 teaspoon ground coriander and 30 g (1 oz) freshly chopped coriander to the flour. Just before cooking, sprinkle the tortilla with a few crushed red chilli flakes.

pitta bread

see base recipe page 144

multi-seed pitta bread
Prepare the basic recipe, adding 2 teaspoons each of sesame seeds, poppy seeds and linseed to the flour.

pitta bread open ham sandwiches
Prepare basic recipe. Spread pitta breads with a little pesto, top each one with a slice of mozzarella, add wafer-thin sliced ham and fold it up slightly. Add another, smaller slice of mozzarella and finish with freshly ground black pepper. Grill for 3–4 minutes until melted and golden.

pitta bread chips
Prepare the basic recipe. Brush both sides of the pitta breads with olive oil and tear into bite-size pieces. Sprinkle with a little ground cumin and coriander, and a few crushed red chilli flakes, and bake at 180°C (350°F) for 10 minutes, until crisp. Sprinkle with salt.

pitta bread with cumin & coriander
Prepare the basic recipe, adding 2 teaspoons ground cumin and 1 tablespoon chopped coriander to the flour.

carly's middle-eastern flatbread

see base recipe page 145

parsley, thyme & fennel flatbread

Prepare the basic recipe, adding 1 tablespoon chopped parsley, 1 teaspoon dried thyme and 1 teaspoon fennel seeds to the flour.

rosemary flatbread

Prepare the basic recipe, adding 1 tablespoon chopped fresh rosemary leaves to the flour.

hummus for flatbread

Prepare the basic recipe and serve with a hummus dip. In a food processor, blend together one 400 g (14 oz) tin chickpeas, rinsed and drained, with olive oil and lemon juice to taste, and a little water if necessary. Add 2 finely chopped spring onions, 2 skinned, seeded and chopped tomatoes, and ½ teaspoon paprika. Serve with flatbread.

rosemary & olive oil flatbread

see base recipe page 146

spicy chilli paste for flatbread
Prepare the basic recipe. Instead of olive oil and rosemary, spread on 1 teaspoon of chilli paste as you take the flatbread out of the frying pan. With a pestle and mortar, mix together 2 chopped cloves of garlic, 1 large seeded and chopped green chilli, 2 teaspoons each of sesame seeds and ground coriander and 2 tablespoons each of olive oil and freshly chopped coriander.

sesame flatbread
Prepare the basic recipe, adding 2 tablespoons sesame seeds to the flour.

red onion, tomato & rosemary flatbread
Prepare the basic recipe, omitting the olive oil and rosemary. Fry 2 thinly sliced red onions in 1 tablespoon olive oil until softened. Add half to the flour in the bowl. Finely chop the leaves from 5–6 rosemary sprigs and add to the remaining onions. Add to the top of the flatbread with 150 g (6 oz) cherry tomatoes as they come out of the frying pan.

variations

salami, tomato & basil pizza

see base recipe page 149

puttanesca pizza
Prepare the basic crust. Spread each pizza base with 4 tablespoons pizza sauce, and add 1 chopped clove of garlic, 6 anchovies, 1 tablespoon capers, 30 g (1 oz) olives, 100 g (4 oz) grated mozzarella and 1 tablespoon freshly chopped parsley before baking.

crispy bacon, mozzarella & black olive pizza
Prepare the basic crust. Spread each pizza base with 4 tablespoons pizza sauce, and add 6 slices of bacon, cooked until crispy and broken, 100 g (4 oz) sliced mozzarella and a few pitted black olives.

roast cherry tomato & cheddar pizza
Prepare the basic crust. Spread each pizza base with 4 tablespoons pizza sauce, and add 60 g (2 oz) grated cheddar cheese, a few cherry tomatoes and another 60 g (2 oz) grated cheddar cheese.

red onion, courgette & rosemary pizza
Prepare the basic crust. Spread each pizza base with 4 tablespoons pizza sauce, and add 3 tablespoons sautéed red onion slices, 6 thin slices courgette and 2 teaspoons chopped fresh rosemary leaves. Add 85 g (3 oz) grated cheddar cheese on top.

variations

sourdough crust with sausage, pepper & mushrooms

see base recipe page 150

sliced tomato & 4-cheese pizza
Prepare the basic crust. Spread each pizza base with 4 tablespoons pizza sauce, and add 1 sliced tomato. Mix together 85 g (3 oz) grated mozzarella, 30 g (1 oz) grated Monterey Jack and 30 g (1 oz) grated Asiago. Spread over the pizza, sprinkle with 15 g (½ oz) grated Pecorino, and drizzle with a little olive oil.

upside-down prosciutto, cheddar & mushroom pizza
Prepare the basic crust. Spread each pizza base with 100 g (4 oz) grated cheddar cheese, 4 slices prosciutto, 2 tablespoons roasted red pepper slices and 2 tablespoons sautéed mushroom slices, and cover with about 8 tablespoons pizza sauce. Bake for an extra 5 minutes, making sure the crust is cooked.

ham & mozzarella bianco pizza
Prepare the basic crust. Spread each pizza base with 4 tablespoons béchamel sauce, and top with 4 slices Serrano ham and 100 g (4 oz) grated mozzarella.

pesto, tomato & goat's cheese pizza
Prepare the basic crust. Spread each pizza base with 4 tablespoons pesto, and add 3 sliced tomatoes, 100 g (4 oz) diced goat's cheese and a drizzle of olive oil. Garnish with fresh basil.

variations

express stuffed-crust pepperoni pizza

see base recipe page 152

express stuffed-crust hot dog pizza
Prepare the basic crust. Spread the pizza base with 4 tablespoons pizza sauce, and add
60 g (2 oz) grated cheddar cheese, 3 tablespoons sautéed mushroom slices, 4 mini hot dogs,
halved, and another 60 g (2 oz) grated cheddar cheese.

express stuffed-crust cajun chicken & chilli pizza
Prepare the basic crust. Spread the pizza base with 4 tablespoons pizza sauce, and add
100 g (4 oz) Cajun-seasoned cooked chicken, 100 g (4 oz) grated mozzarella and a sprinkling
of crushed red chilli flakes.

express stuffed-crust parma ham & tomato pizza
Prepare the basic crust. Spread the pizza base with 4 tablespoons pizza sauce, add 4 slices
Parma ham and 2 sliced tomatoes, and cover with 85 g (3 oz) grated cheddar cheese.

express stuffed-crust mexican bean & jack pizza
Prepare the basic crust. Mix 5 tablespoons pizza sauce with 100 g (4 oz) tinned red kidney
beans, drained, and 1 crushed clove of garlic, ½ teaspoon chilli powder and 2 tablespoons
chopped coriander. Spread it over the pizza base, cover with 85 g (3 oz) grated Monterey Jack
cheese, and garnish with fresh rocket.

variations

yeast-free chilli seafood pizza

see base recipe page 153

sweet italian sausage, mushroom & basil pizza
Prepare the basic crust. Spread the pizza base with 4 tablespoons pizza sauce, and add
60 g (2 oz) grated cheddar cheese, 100 g (4 oz) cooked and crumbled Italian sausage and
2 tablespoons sautéed mushroom slices. Top with another 60 g (2 oz) grated cheddar cheese.
Garnish with 6 fresh basil leaves.

ham & pineapple pizza
Prepare the basic crust. Spread the pizza base with 4 tablespoons pizza sauce, and add
60 g (2 oz) grated cheddar cheese, 100 g (4 oz) thinly sliced ham, and 60 g (2 oz) chopped
pineapple. Top with another 85 g (3 oz) grated cheddar cheese.

onion, pepperoni, mushroom & pepper pizza
Prepare the basic crust. Spread the pizza base with 4 tablespoons pizza sauce, and add
60 g (2 oz) grated cheddar cheese, 3 tablespoons sautéed onion slices, 10 slices of pepperoni,
2 tablespoons sautéed mushroom slices and 2 tablespoons roasted red pepper slices. Top with
85 g (3 oz) grated mozzarella.

sliced tomato & olive pizza
Prepare the basic crust. Spread the pizza base with 3 sliced tomatoes, scatter over a handful
of pitted black olives and top with 100 g (4 oz) mozzarella, sliced.

variations

gluten-free spinach, basil & mozzarella pizza

see base recipe page 154

gluten-free courgette, cherry tomato & brie pizza
Prepare the basic crust. Spread each pizza base with 4 tablespoons pizza sauce, 6 thin slices courgette, 6 cherry tomatoes and 85 g (3 oz) Brie, sliced. Garnish with 6 basil leaves.

gluten-free king prawn, spinach & mozzarella pizza
Prepare the basic crust. Spread each pizza with 60 g (2 oz) king prawns, 30 g (1 oz) wilted spinach leaves and 85 g (3 oz) mozzarella, sliced.

gluten-free meat feast, chilli & cheddar pizza
Prepare the basic crust. Spread each pizza base with 4 tablespoons pizza sauce, and add 85 g (3 oz) Cajun-seasoned cooked chicken, 6 slices pepperoni and 3 slices bacon, cooked until crispy. Top with a seeded and finely chopped red chilli and 85 g (3 oz) mixed grated mozzarella and cheddar cheese.

gluten-free margherita pizza
Prepare the basic crust. Spread each pizza base with 4 tablespoons pizza sauce, and add 60 g (2 oz) grated mozzarella cheese, 1 tablespoon finely grated Parmesan cheese, a few halved cherry tomatoes and 2 tablespoons freshly chopped basil to each one.

variations

polenta pan pizza with oven-roasted mediterranean vegetables

see base recipe page 157

sausage, mushroom & bacon pan pizza
Prepare the basic recipe. Omit the topping, and top with 100 g (4 oz) cooked and crumbled Italian sausage, 85 g (3 oz) sautéed mushrooms and 3 slices of bacon, cooked until crispy and halved. Put back under the grill for 3–4 minutes and garnish with 6 basil leaves.

fresh spinach, goat's cheese & cherry tomato pan pizza
Prepare the basic recipe. Omit the topping and spread the crust with 2 tablespoons pizza sauce, 30 g (1 oz) fresh spinach leaves, 85 g (3 oz) goat's cheese, sliced and 6 cherry tomatoes. Put back under the grill for 3–4 minutes and garnish with 6 basil leaves.

mozzarella, anchovy, caper & parsley pan pizza
Prepare the basic recipe. Omit the topping and spread the crust with 2 tablespoons pizza sauce, 6 good-quality anchovies, 1 seeded and chopped red chilli, 1 tablespoon drained capers, and 100 g (4 oz) grated mozzarella. Place back under the grill for 3–4 minutes, and garnish with 2 tablespoons freshly chopped parsley.

smoked pancetta, mozzarella, fresh chilli & tomato pan pizza
Prepare the basic recipe. Omit the topping and top with 3 tablespoons pizza sauce, 85 g (3 oz) chopped pancetta, 85 g (3 oz) grated mozzarella, 1 sliced tomato and 1 seeded and chopped red chilli. Place back under the grill for 3–4 minutes, garnish with freshly chopped coriander.

variations

parmesan & garlic breadsticks

see base recipe page 158

crispy breadsticks
Prepare the basic recipe. Cut the dough into 1.5-cm (½-in) strips instead of 2.5-cm (1-in) strips. Bake for 40 minutes at 150°C (300°F), until they are crispy.

bacon-wrapped breadsticks
Prepare the basic recipe. Cut 6 slices of bacon in half, so that they are about 12.5 cm (5 in) long. Wrap 1 slice around each breadstick and bake on baking-paper-lined baking sheets at 180°C (350°F), until the bacon has browned. Roll in Parmesan cheese mixed with garlic pepper seasoning.

pizza-seasoned breadsticks
Prepare the basic recipe. Sprinkle the tops with pizza seasoning. Mix together 2 tablespoons oregano, 1 teaspoon dried basil, 1 teaspoon lemon pepper and ½ teaspoon each of dried thyme, salt, fennel, onion powder and paprika.

jalapeño breadsticks
Prepare the basic recipe. Just before sprinkling with garlic salt, lay slices of jalapeño across the breadsticks, either fresh or from a jar.

variations

sundried tomato & olive sticks

see base recipe page 160

date & blue cheese sticks
Prepare the basic recipe, replacing the olives with 30 g (1 oz) finely chopped dried dates. Add 60 g (2 oz) crumbled blue cheese to the bowl with the flour.

breadsticks with curry seasoning
Prepare the basic recipe, omitting the olives. Add 2 teaspoons hot curry powder to the bowl with the flour.

fajita-seasoned breadsticks
Prepare the basic recipe, omitting the olives. Add 1 tablespoon fajita seasoning to the bowl with the flour, and sprinkle on more just before baking (see tortilla variation recipe page 162).

poppy & pumpkin seed breadsticks
Prepare the basic recipe, omitting the sundried tomatoes and olives. Add 30 g (1 oz) poppy seeds and 60 g (2 oz) pumpkin seeds to the bowl with the flour. Just before baking, gently brush each breadstick with a little butter and sprinkle generously with more poppy seeds.

meals in a loaf

In this chapter, you will find a variety of ideas for enclosing your breakfast or lunch in a bread roll or loaf, which makes it not only fun, but very easy to enjoy on the go.

mustard corn dogs

see variations page 188

With a little kick of cayenne and the slight tang of buttermilk, this recipe is reminiscent of the traditional treat at county fairs.

125 g (4¹/₂ oz) plain flour
100 g (3¹/₂ oz) polenta
2 tbsp sugar
1 tsp baking powder
¹/₄ tsp baking soda
¹/₂ tsp dry mustard
¹/₂ tsp cayenne
1 tsp salt

55 ml (2 fl oz) buttermilk
1 egg, room temperature, lightly beaten
180 ml (6 fl oz) whole milk
8 medium hot dogs
8 bamboo skewers, soaked, or 8 chopsticks
about 1 litre (2 pints) canola or sunflower oil
mustard and ketchup to serve

In a large bowl, combine the flour, polenta, sugar, baking powder, baking soda, dry mustard, cayenne and salt. Make a well in the centre, and add the buttermilk, beaten egg and enough milk to make a thick batter. Set aside.

Pour oil to a depth of 5 cm (2 in) into an large, deep-sided pan and heat over medium-high heat until a deep-fry thermometer reads 180°C (350°F). Skewer 1 hot dog with a bamboo skewer or chopstick, and dip into batter so that the hot dog is completely covered. Transfer quickly to the Dutch oven and fry in the hot oil for about 3 minutes, until golden brown. Using tongs, remove the corn dog to drain on paper towels, and repeat with remaining hot dogs and batter. Serve immediately with mustard and ketchup, if desired.

Makes 12 rolls

soup in a roll

see variations page 189

Soup bowls are best used for thicker, chowder-type soups, as thin soups might seep through the bread.

2 tsp active dry yeast
300 ml (10 fl oz) warm water
450 g (1 lb) white bread flour
1 tsp salt

1 tbsp polenta for sprinkling
1 egg white
1 tbsp water
oil for greasing

Lightly grease a large baking sheet with a little oil and sprinkle with polenta. Dissolve the yeast in the warm water and set aside for 10–15 minutes, until creamy. In a large bowl, combine the flour and salt. Make a well in the centre and pour in the yeast liquid. Mix until a dough comes together. Knead for about 10 minutes, until the dough is soft, smooth and elastic. Place the dough in a large lightly oiled bowl, cover and put in a warm place for an hour or so, until doubled in size. Turn the dough out on to a lightly floured work surface and punch down. Divide into four equal portions. Shape each one into a 10-cm (4-in) round loaf and place on the baking sheet. Place inside a greased plastic bag and leave for about 35 minutes, until doubled in size.

Preheat the oven to 200°C (400°F). In a small bowl, beat the egg white and water together, and brush half of it over the dough. Bake for 15 minutes, brush with the rest of the egg white and bake for another 10–15 minutes, until golden brown. Cool on a wire rack. Cut a 1.5-cm (1/2-in)-thick slice from the top of each loaf and scoop out the centres, leaving 2-cm (3/4-in)-thick shells. Fill with hot and creamy soup (see variations page 189) and serve.

Makes 4 bread bowls

chicken & ham brioche rolls

see variations page 190

These rolls, which hide a yummy chicken and ham filling, make a great lunch-to-go.

1 tsp + 1 tbsp sugar, divided
240 ml (8 fl oz) warm milk
2 tsp active dry yeast
575 g (1 lb 4½ oz) white bread flour
1 tsp salt
2 eggs, room temperature, lightly beaten
2 tbsp unsalted butter, melted and cooled
oil for greasing
225 g (8 oz) grated cheddar cheese

60 g (2 oz) cream cheese, room temperature
100 g (4 oz) each cooked ham and
   chicken, diced
60 g (2 oz) grated mozzarella
6 spring onions, finely chopped
2 tomatoes, seeded and chopped
2 tsp Dijon mustard
1 egg, beaten
2 tbsp grated Parmesan cheese

Grease a 12-hole muffin tin with a little oil. Dissolve 1 teaspoon sugar in the warm milk, sprinkle the yeast on top and leave for 10–15 minutes until frothy. In a large bowl, mix the flour, salt and remaining sugar together. Make a well in the centre, and add the yeast liquid, eggs and butter. With a wooden spoon, mix and then beat the dough until it leaves the side of the bowl clean. On a lightly floured work surface, knead for 5 minutes, until smooth and elastic. Place in a large lightly oiled bowl, cover and leave at room temperature for an hour or so, until doubled in size. Turn the dough out on to a lightly floured work surface and knead for 2 minutes, until smooth. Mix filling ingredients together. Put a dough circle in each of the muffin holes, push in lightly and fill each one with a little filling. Pinch the tops of the dough together roughly to make little parcels. Cover, and leave in a warm place for 45 minutes, until almost doubled in size. Preheat the oven to 180°C (350°F). Brush with beaten egg, and sprinkle with Parmesan. Bake for 25–30 minutes, until golden brown. Serve warm, or cool on a rack.

Makes 12 rolls

stuffed veggie loaf

see variations page 191

Filling and wholesome, I defy anyone not to absolutely love this lunchtime treat!

1 tsp sugar dissolved in 240 ml (8 fl oz) warm water
2 tsp active dry yeast
385 g (13$^{1}/_{2}$ oz) white bread flour
1 tsp salt
2 tbsp sugar
60 ml (2 fl oz) + 2 tbsp olive oil
1 large onion, finely chopped
4 cloves garlic, finely chopped

$^{1}/_{4}$ tsp chilli powder
1 tsp ground coriander
$^{1}/_{2}$ tsp garam masala
2 green chillies, seeded and finely chopped
1 large potato, peeled, diced and parboiled
1 large carrot, peeled, diced and parboiled
4 tbsp tinned red kidney beans, crushed
30 g (1 oz) cooked and drained spinach

Sprinkle the yeast into the sugar–water mix, and set aside for 10–15 minutes, until frothy. In a large bowl, combine the flour, salt and 2 tablespoons sugar. Make a well in the centre, pour in the yeast liquid, add 60 ml (2 fl oz) olive oil and mix until a dough begins to form. Knead for about 10 minutes to make a silky dough. Transfer the dough to a large lightly oiled bowl and turn to coat it all over. Cover and put in a warm place for an hour or so, until doubled in size. While the dough is proving, make the filling. In a large frying pan, heat the oil and sauté the onion for 5 minutes, until soft. Add the garlic, chilli powder, coriander and garam masala, and cook for 2 minutes. Add the remaining ingredients and cook for a further 5 minutes. Set aside to cool. Preheat the oven to 200°C (400°F). Turn the dough out on to a lightly floured work surface and punch down. Press flat and roll out to a large rectangle. Place the filling down the centre, and fold up the sides. Lift on to a lined baking sheet, brush with beaten egg and bake for about 35 minutes, until golden brown. Cool on a wire rack, or serve hot.

Makes 1 loaf

full english loaf

see variations page 192

This bread has all the flavours of a full English fried breakfast wrapped up in a convenient sandwich loaf.

510 g (1 lb 2 oz) white bread flour
2 tsp salt
1 tbsp instant dry yeast
60 ml (2 fl oz) olive oil
320 ml (11 fl oz) warm water

6 strips bacon, cooked until crispy,
and crumbled
4 cooked sausage links, chopped
2 hard-boiled eggs, chopped
2 large Roma tomatoes, seeded and chopped

Place the flour in a large bowl, and add the salt on one side and the yeast on the other. Make a well in the centre, and add the olive oil and three-quarters of the warm water. Gradually add the rest of the water until the mixture comes together as a soft but not soggy dough. Turn the dough out on to a lightly floured work surface and knead for 10 minutes until silky and elastic. Put the dough into a large lightly oiled bowl and turn to coat it all over. Cover and leave in a warm place for an hour or so, until doubled in size. Turn the dough out on to a lightly floured work surface and gently press it into a rectangle, about 35 x 30 cm (14 x 12 in), trying not to knock out the air bubbles. Sprinkle the bacon, sausage, egg and tomato over the dough and roll up from the long side. Curve it around into a spiral and place on a lined baking sheet. Cover and leave at room temperature for an hour or so until the dough has at least doubled in size. Preheat the oven to 220°C (425°F) and place a large roasting tin on the lowest shelf. When the dough has risen, fill the roasting tin halfway with hot water and place the dough on a higher shelf in the oven. Bake for about 30 minutes, or until golden brown and the bottom of the loaf sounds hollow when tapped. Cool on a wire rack.

Makes 1 loaf

jalapeño, bacon & cheddar cornbread

see variations page 193

First made by Native Americans, cornbread has evolved and can be made very simply or, like this recipe, with lots of interesting flavours.

90 g (3¼ oz) plain flour
140 g (5 oz) polenta
50 g (2 oz) sugar
1 tbsp baking powder
½ tsp bicarbonate of soda
½ tsp salt
1 egg, room temperature, lightly beaten
240 ml (8 fl oz) whole milk

50 g (2 oz) butter, melted and cooled + extra
    for greasing
6 slices bacon, cooked until crispy, and
    crumbled
2 tbsp honey
1 jalapeño, finely chopped
175 g (6 oz) grated cheddar cheese

Preheat the oven to 220°C (425°F) and lightly grease a 20 x 20-cm (8 x 8-in) baking dish with a little butter. In a large bowl, combine the flour, polenta, sugar, baking powder, bicarbonate of soda and salt. Set aside. In a medium bowl, blend together the egg, milk and melted butter. Make a well in the centre of the flour mixture, and add the milk mixture and crumbled bacon. Fold together lightly until just combined, and transfer to the baking dish. Drizzle the honey over the top, and sprinkle with the jalapeño and cheddar cheese. Bake for 20–25 minutes, until the top is golden and the cheese is melted and slightly browned. Remove from the oven and cool on a wire rack. Cut into squares and serve warm or cold.

Makes 8 servings

pesto focaccia with ricotta

see variations page 194

For an even more aromatic bread, add a little chopped fresh rosemary to the dough.

255 g (9 oz) white bread flour
$^1/_2$ tsp salt
2 tsp garlic powder
2 tsp Italian dried herbs
1 tsp active dry yeast
180 ml (6 fl oz) warm water
1$^1/_2$ tbsp extra virgin olive oil + extra for
    drizzling and greasing

coarse sea salt for sprinkling

for the filling
5 Roma tomatoes, halved, and roasted with
    1 tbsp olive oil in a hot oven
175 g (6 oz) ricotta cheese
salt and freshly ground black pepper to taste
4 tbsp pesto (see variations recipe page 194)

Line a large baking sheet with baking paper, and lightly grease a 23 x 18-cm (9 x 7-in) rectangular glass baking dish with a little olive oil. In a large bowl, combine the flour, salt, garlic powder and dried herbs. In a small bowl, mix the yeast with 120 ml (4 fl oz) warm water and stir to dissolve the yeast. Set aside for 5 minutes. Make a well in the centre of the flour, and add the yeast liquid and 1$^1/_2$ tablespoons olive oil. Turn the mixture around with either a plastic dough scraper or your hands. Gradually add the rest of the water until a sticky dough is formed. You may not have to use it all. Turn the dough out on to a lightly floured or oiled work surface. Knead the dough for about 10 minutes, until it is smooth and elastic. The dough will be wetter at first, but will form a smooth skin. Transfer to the oiled dish, cover with a kitchen towel and leave to rise in a warm place for an hour or so.

Turn the dough out on to a lightly floured work surface, try not to knock the air out and stretch the dough into a rectangle. Carefully lift on to the baking sheet, place in a greased plastic bag and leave for about an hour, until doubled in size.

Preheat the oven to 220°C (425°F). Remove the baking sheet from the plastic bag and make deep dimples in the dough with your fingers. Drizzle the focaccia with 1–2 tablespoons olive oil and sprinkle with coarse sea salt. Push small rosemary sprigs into the dough. Bake for 15 minutes, or until the top is golden brown and the bottom of the loaf sounds hollow when tapped. Cool on a wire rack. Cut the focaccia in half horizontally and lightly grill each cut side. In a small bowl, season the ricotta cheese with salt and freshly ground black pepper. Spread the cut side of the bottom half of the focaccia with ricotta and lay the tomatoes on top. Spread the cut side of the top half of the focaccia with pesto, and sandwich the two together. Cut into wedges and serve immediately.

Makes 6 servings

deep-fried vegetable rolls

see variations page 195

Try serving these delicious rolls hot, with sweet chili sauce for dipping.

1 tbsp olive oil
1 tsp cumin seeds
1 large onion, finely chopped
2 cloves garlic, crushed
2 green chillies, seeded and finely chopped
1 tbsp fresh ginger, finely chopped
1 tsp ground coriander
1/2 tsp garam masala
1 tsp curry powder

1/4 tsp turmeric
200 g (7 oz) tinned black-eyed peas, well
    drained and crushed
30 g (1 oz) freshly chopped coriander
salt and freshly ground black pepper to taste
8 large slices bread
cornflour
1 tbsp vegetable oil for deep frying

In a large frying pan, heat 1 tablespoon olive oil and fry the cumin seeds for 1 minute.
Add the chopped onion and garlic, and sauté over a medium-low heat for 5 minutes, until
softened. Add the chillies, ginger and spices, and continue to cook for 3 minutes. Add the
crushed black-eyed peas and chopped coriander, and stir well. Cook on low for about
5 minutes, remove from the heat and set aside to cool. Season with salt and freshly ground
black pepper. Quickly dip the slices of bread in and out of a shallow dish of cold water, and
squeeze the water out with your hands. Lay the bread slices on the work surface and place
about 2 tablespoons of the filling in the middle of the slices. Wrap the bread around the
filling, enclosing it completely, and dust each one with cornflour. If you have time, chill the
rolls in the fridge for 30 minutes. Heat the oil, and when it is hot but not smoking, deep-fry
the rolls for 3–5 minutes, or until they are deep golden. Drain on kitchen paper and keep
warm while you fry all the rolls. Serve hot.

Makes 8 rolls

chilli chicken stromboli

see variations page 196

This is a great way to use up leftover chicken. Spice it up with chillies and tomatoes, add cheese, and you get a winning combination.

340 g (12 oz) boneless cold cooked chicken
2 green chillies, seeded and finely chopped
100 g (4 oz) cream cheese, room temperature
60 g (2 oz) chopped roasted, skinned and
    seeded red pepper
1 tbsp honey
1 recipe white bread dough (see recipe page 17)

6 tbsp pizza sauce (see recipe page 150)
1 egg, lightly beaten
2 tbsp freshly chopped parsley
6 thin strips roasted, skinned and seeded
    red pepper
1 tbsp butter, melted + extra for greasing
garlic powder for sprinkling

Preheat the oven to 180°C (350°F) and grease a large baking sheet with a little butter. In a large bowl, mix the chicken, chillies, cream cheese, 60 g (2 oz) red pepper and honey together. After leaving the white bread dough to rise, turn it out on to a lightly floured work surface and punch down. Roll it out slightly, and leave to rest for 10 minutes. Roll the dough out to a 38 x 25-cm (15 x 10-in) rectangle, and spread the pizza sauce over the dough, leaving a small border. Spread the chicken mixture over the sauce. Tuck the short sides of the rectangle in, and roll up the long side like a Swiss roll. Lift on to the baking sheet, seam underneath, and brush with the beaten egg. Sprinkle with chopped parsley, and lay the strips of red pepper over the top of the loaf, about 5 cm (2 in) apart. With a sharp knife, cut five or six diagonal slices, 1.5 cm (1/2 in) deep on top of the loaf. Bake for 25–30 minutes, until the loaf is golden brown. Remove from the oven, brush the top of the loaf with melted butter and sprinkle with garlic powder.

Makes 6 servings

meatballs in garlic bread

see variations page 197

These little rolls make excellent appetisers or an after-school snack. Dip them in pizza sauce for a crowd- or child-pleaser.

1 recipe traditional dinner
    rolls (see recipe page 249)
675 g (1¹/₂ lb) lean minced beef
40 g (1¹/₂ oz) breadcrumbs
1 large onion, finely chopped
1 clove garlic, crushed
1 tbsp Worcestershire sauce

1 tbsp soy sauce
2 tsp Italian dried herbs
2 tsp beef bouillon
1 egg, lightly beaten
35 g (1¹/₃ oz) plain flour
2 tbsp olive oil
3 tbsp garlic powder

150 g (5¹/₂ oz) mozzarella,
    sliced
1 egg, beaten
3 tbsp freshly chopped parsley
500 ml (2 pints) pizza sauce,
    blended, for dipping (see
    recipe page 150)

Make the dough as directed in the traditional dinner rolls recipe, and leave to rise. Make the meatballs. In a large bowl, stir together the beef, breadcrumbs, onion, garlic, Worcestershire sauce, soy sauce, herbs, beef bouillon and egg. Mix well, form into 15 meatballs and roll each one in flour. In a large frying pan, heat 2 tablespoons olive oil and fry the meatballs, turning them around until they are browned all over and are cooked through, about 10–15 minutes. Drain on kitchen paper. After rising the dough, turn it out on to a lightly floured work surface and punch down. Divide it into 15 equal portions and form into balls. Roll each as thinly as possible into a circle, and sprinkle with a little garlic powder. Place a meatball on each one, add a slice of mozzarella cheese, and roll the dough around the meatballs to enclose them completely. Pinch the edges together to seal completely. Place the rolls on a baking sheet, join underneath, cover with cling film and leave to rest for 10 minutes. Remove the cover, brush with beaten egg, sprinkle with freshly chopped parsley and bake for about 20 minutes, until golden brown. Serve immediately with pizza sauce on the side.

Makes 15 rolls

variations

mustard corn dogs

see base recipe page 175

mini vegetarian corn dogs
Prepare the basic recipe, replacing the hot dogs with mini vegetarian dogs. Instead of the sticks, use tongs to batter and deep-fry.

cheese corn dogs
Prepare the basic recipe, replacing the hot dogs with fingers of hard cheese, such as cheddar, slightly smaller than the hot dogs.

corn dogs with Italian sausage
Prepare the basic recipe, replacing the hot dogs with Italian sausages, cooked and cooled.

apple slice doughnuts
Prepare the basic recipe, replacing the mustard and cayenne with 2 tablespoons sugar. Replace the hot dogs with thick slices of peeled and cored apple. Instead of sticks, use tongs to batter and deep-fry. Sprinkle with cinnamon and sugar to serve.

variations

soup in a roll

see base recipe page 176

creamy squash soup in herbed bread bowls
Prepare the basic recipe. Make soup by cooking 1 large seeded and chopped butternut
squash, 1 finely chopped onion, 1 peeled and chopped carrot, 1 teaspoon ground cumin and
salt and freshly ground black pepper in 1.25 l (2½ pints) chicken or vegetable stock until
tender. Blend until smooth. Reheat, fill bowls and garnish with chopped coriander.

chilli in a roll
Prepare the basic recipe, replacing the filling with your favourite chilli recipe.

chicken alfredo pasta in a roll
Prepare the basic recipe. Melt 1 teaspoon olive oil and 60 g (2 oz) butter over medium heat
and fry 1 skinless chicken breast (chopped) until browned. Add 240 g (8 oz) cream cheese,
2 teaspoons garlic powder, 500 ml (1 pint) milk, 170 g (6 oz) grated Parmesan cheese and
freshly ground black pepper. Toss with fettuccini and fill bowls. Garnish with chopped parsley.

artichoke & spinach dip in a roll
Prepare the basic recipe. In a medium bowl, combine 200 g (7 oz) mayonnaise, 170 g (6 oz)
grated Parmesan cheese, one 400-g (14-oz) tin drained artichoke hearts, 100 g (4 oz) washed
and chopped spinach, and 1 tablespoon chilli sauce. Transfer to a shallow greased baking
dish and bake at 170°C (325°F) for 35–40 minutes until browned. Transfer to the bread bowls
and garnish with chopped parsley.

variations

chicken & ham brioche rolls

see base recipe page 178

roasted mediterranean vegetable brioche rolls
Prepare the basic recipe, replacing the filling with 680 g (1½ lb) of mixed roasted mediterranean vegetables.

pulled pork brioche rolls
Prepare the basic recipe, replacing the filling with 450 g (1 lb) pulled pork, mixed with barbecue sauce, to taste.

breakfast brioche rolls
Prepare the basic recipe, replacing the filling with 8 slices of bacon, cooked until crispy and crumbled, mixed with 4 chopped eggs, 4 chopped tomatoes, 6 chopped sausage links and ketchup, to taste.

mushroom & shallot brioche rolls
Prepare the basic recipe, replacing the filling with (450 g (1 lb) sliced mushrooms and 4 finely chopped shallots, poached together in vegetable bouillon until tender.

stuffed veggie loaf

see base recipe page 179

lamb in a loaf
Prepare the basic recipe, replacing the filling with 450 g (1 lb) minced lamb cooked with
1 onion, 1 crushed clove of garlic and 2 teaspoons garam masala, and seasoned with salt and
freshly ground black pepper.

roasted mediterranean veggies in a loaf
Prepare the basic recipe, replacing the filling with 450 g (1 lb) roasted
Mediterranean vegetables.

moroccan-spiced veggie loaf
Prepare the basic recipe, replacing the chilli powder, ground coriander and garam masala
with 2 teaspoons Moroccan spice flavouring. Mix 2 teaspoons each of ground nutmeg, cumin
and coriander. Add 1 teaspoon each of mixed spice and ground ginger, and ½ teaspoon each
of cayenne pepper and cinnamon. Store excess in a jar with a lid for up to 1 week.

sausage & beans in a loaf
Prepare the basic recipe, replacing the filling with 4 chopped cold sausage links mixed with
half a 400-g (14-oz) tin baked beans in tomato sauce.

variations

full english loaf

see base recipe page 180

bacon, cheese & onion loaf
Prepare the basic recipe, replacing the sausages with 120 g (4$\frac{1}{2}$ oz) grated cheddar cheese sprinkled over the rest of the filling.

maple, raisin & pecan loaf
Prepare the basic recipe, omitting the filling. Substitute 170 g (6 oz) raisins soaked in 1 tablespoon maple syrup and 170 g (6 oz) chopped pecans. Sprinkle on 75 g (2$\frac{1}{2}$ oz) brown sugar before rolling up.

sausage & bean loaf
Prepare the basic recipe, omitting the bacon and adding another 3 chopped sausage links. Add half a 400-g (14-oz) tin baked beans in tomato sauce before rolling up.

ham & swiss loaf
Prepare the basic recipe. Omit the bacon, sausage and chopped eggs from the filling and replace with 170 g (6 oz) ham, finely chopped, and 170 g (6 oz) grated Swiss cheese, sprinkled over the ham.

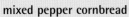

variations

jalapeño, bacon & cheddar cornbread

see base recipe page 181

mixed pepper cornbread
Prepare the basic recipe, adding 40 g (1½ oz) cooked and finely chopped mixed peppers to the bowl with the flour.

asparagus, bacon & cheddar cornbread
Prepare the basic recipe, adding 8 finely sliced asparagus spears to the bowl with the flour.

broccoli, ham & cheddar cornbread
Prepare the basic recipe, adding 85 g (3 oz) steamed broccoli florets to the mixture with the milk mixture. Replace the bacon with 100 g (4 oz) ham, finely chopped.

onion, bacon & cheddar cornbread
Prepare the basic recipe, adding 4 finely chopped spring onions to the mixture with the bacon.

variations

pesto focaccia with ricotta

see base recipe page 182

pesto focaccia with chargrilled aubergine, feta & sweet potato

Prepare the basic recipe, omitting the ricotta cheese. Spread 100 g (4 oz) sweet potato purée over half of the focaccia and add sliced tomatoes, 170 g (6 oz) crumbled feta cheese and 4 slices chargrilled aubergine to the other half on top of the pesto. Sandwich the halves together as directed.

pesto focaccia with ricotta, goat's cheese & salami

Prepare the basic recipe. Add 100 g (4 oz) chopped goat's cheese to the ricotta cheese and tomatoes, and lay a few slices of salami on top. Sandwich together with the other half with the pesto.

pesto focaccia with chicken, avocado & swiss cheese

Prepare the basic recipe, omitting the ricotta cheese. Place 1 avocado, stoned and sliced, on top of the tomatoes, then add 170 g (6 oz) cooked sliced chicken, and sprinkle 100 g (4 oz) grated Swiss cheese on top. Sandwich together with the other half with the pesto.

pesto focaccia with cream cheese, smoked salmon & rocket

Prepare the basic recipe, replacing the ricotta cheese with cream cheese. Replace tomatoes with a layer of thinly sliced smoked salmon. Add 50 g (2 oz) rocket and sandwich together with the other half without the pesto.

deep-fried vegetable rolls

see base recipe page 184

deep-fried potato, onion & garam masala rolls
Prepare the basic recipe, replacing the beans in the filling with 200 g (7 oz) cooked diced potatoes.

deep-fried chicken & coriander rolls
Prepare the basic recipe, replacing the beans in the filling with 200 g (7 oz) chicken and 2 tablespoons chopped coriander.

deep-fried sweet potato & pecan rolls
Prepare the basic recipe, replacing the filling with 200 g (7 oz) cooked diced sweet potato mixed with 60 g (2 oz) chopped pecans and 60 g (2 oz) brown sugar.

deep-fried sweet & nutty rolls
Prepare the basic recipe, omitting the filling. Substitute 200 g (7 oz) finely chopped nuts mixed with 25 g (³/₄ oz) flaked coconut and 75 g (2¹/₂ oz) brown sugar combined and bound together with 85 g (3 oz) melted dark chocolate.

variations

chilli chicken stromboli

see base recipe page 185

ham & swiss cheese stromboli
Prepare the basic recipe, omitting the filling. Spread on the pizza sauce and add 4–5 slices wafer-thin ham and sprinkle over 100 g (4 oz) grated Swiss cheese. Proceed as directed.

feta cheese, pepper & caramelised onion stromboli
Prepare the basic recipe, omitting the filling. Spread on the pizza sauce and add 100 g (4 oz) crumbled feta cheese, 40 g (1½ oz) sliced and cooked pepper and 60 g (2 oz) cooked caramelised onions. Proceed as directed.

pepperoni calzone
Prepare the basic recipe, omitting the pizza sauce. Make a new filling by mixing together 200 g (7 oz) pepperoni, 100 g (4 oz) grated mozzarella, 8 halved cherry tomatoes, 1 tablespoon drained capers and 30 g (1 oz) grated Parmesan cheese. Roll the dough out to a circle 42 cm (15 in) in diameter and spread the filling on to one half of the dough. Slightly wet the outside edge and fold half over to meet the other side. Seal. Proceed as directed.

sausage, mushroom & bacon stromboli
Prepare the basic recipe and make a new filling. Mix together 4 slices of bacon, cooked until crispy and crumbled, 170 g (6 oz) cooked sausagemeat, well drained, and 40 g (1½ oz) sautéed mushrooms. Add the filling to the pizza sauce and proceed as directed.

variations

meatballs in garlic bread

see base recipe page 187

moroccan lamb meatballs in garlic bread
Prepare the basic recipe. Replace the minced beef with minced lamb, omit the Italian dried
herbs in the meat and substitute 3 teaspoons Moroccan spice mix (see recipe for stuffed
veggie loaf variations, page 191).

nut loaf balls in garlic bread
Prepare the basic recipe. Make nut loaf meatballs. Roast 200 g (7 oz) mixed nuts (not
peanuts) at 180°C (350°F) for 10 minutes. Pulse in a food processor until ground but still
with texture. Sauté 1 finely chopped onion, 1 crushed clove of garlic and 1 grated carrot for
2 minutes; add 3 skinned, seeded and chopped tomatoes, and season. Transfer to a bowl and
cool. Add the nuts, 120 g (4½ oz) breadcrumbs, 100 g (4 oz) grated Swiss cheese,
2 tablespoons mixed herbs and 2 beaten eggs. Roll into balls and fry for 3–4 minutes.
Proceed as directed.

ham & eggs in bread
Prepare the basic recipe, replacing the meatballs with a wafer-thin slice of ham wrapped
around ½ a boiled egg inside each roll.

sausage meatballs in garlic bread
Prepare the basic recipe, replacing the beef with minced pork.

sweet bread &
bread desserts

In this chapter, you will find delicious sweetened

loaf recipes as well as exciting ways to make your

home-baked bread into delectable desserts to wow

your friends and family.

caribbean bread pudding

see variations page 215

This is full of pineapple and coconut and, with a decadent hint of rum, ticks all the boxes for a delicious dessert.

500 g (1 lb 2 oz) bread cubes
2 tbsp butter, melted + extra for greasing
25 g (³/₄ oz) grated coconut flakes
40 g (1¹/₂ oz) diced tinned pineapple,
   well drained

4 eggs
100 g (4 oz) sugar
355 ml (12 fl oz) whole milk
1 tsp vanilla extract
2 tbsp coconut rum

Preheat the oven to 180°C (350°F) and generously butter a medium-sized baking dish. Place the bread cubes in a large bowl, pour over the melted butter and stir them together to coat the bread all over. Transfer the cubes to a baking sheet and bake in the oven for about 10 minutes, until nicely toasted. Lower the temperature of the oven to 150°C (300°F).

Transfer the toasted bread cubes to the baking dish and stir in the coconut and pineapple. In a large bowl, whisk together the eggs, sugar, milk, vanilla and rum, and pour over the bread mixture. Press down on the cubes of bread so that they absorb most of the liquid. Bake the dessert in the oven for about an hour, or until it is firm in the centre. Serve warm.

Serves 6

chocolate marbled bread

see variations page 216

The bananas keep this bread very moist, and the swirl of chocolate makes it look lovely when sliced.

255 g (9 oz) plain flour
³/₄ tsp bicarbonate of soda
¹/₂ tsp salt
50 g (2 oz) butter, softened
200 g (7 oz) sugar
3 ripe bananas, mashed

2 eggs, room temperature, lightly beaten
80 ml (3 fl oz) buttermilk
1 tsp vanilla extract
75 g (3 oz) dark chocolate chips
oil for greasing

Preheat the oven to 180°C (350°F) and grease a 450-g (1-lb) 20 x 10-cm (8 x 4-in) loaf tin with a little oil. In a large bowl, combine the flour, bicarbonate of soda and salt. In another bowl, beat the softened butter and sugar together with an electric mixer until creamy. Add the mashed bananas, eggs, buttermilk and vanilla, and beat until just blended. Fold in the flour and lightly stir until just combined.

In a medium microwave-safe bowl, melt the chocolate chips in the microwave until almost melted, and stir until smooth. Cool for 5 minutes, add around 240 ml (8 fl oz) batter to the chocolate chips, and stir until well mixed. Spoon both batters into the loaf tin alternately, and swirl them together slightly with a knife. Bake for 1 hour 15 minutes, or until a cocktail stick inserted into the centre comes out clean. Cool in the tin for 10 minutes, and turn out on to a wire rack to cool completely.

Makes 1 loaf

sweet cornbread with summer berry sauce

see variations page 217

This sweet version of an old favourite makes a great dessert.

140 g (5 oz) polenta
130 g (4½ oz) plain flour
140 g (5 oz) sugar
2 tsp baking powder
½ tsp bicarbonate of soda
½ tsp salt
80 ml (3 fl oz) sunflower oil

3 tbsp butter, melted and
   cooled + extra for greasing
1 tbsp honey
2 eggs, room temperature,
   lightly beaten
240 ml (8 fl oz) buttermilk
100 g (4 oz) strawberries,
   halved if large

100 g (4 oz) blueberries
100 g (4 oz) raspberries
140 g (5 oz) sugar
1 tbsp lemon juice
2 tsp lemon zest
1 tbsp cornflour
2 tbsp water

Preheat the oven to 180°C (350°F) and generously butter a 20 x 20-cm (8 x 8-in) square baking tin. In a large bowl, combine the polenta, flour, sugar, baking powder, bicarbonate of soda and salt. Make a well in the centre and add the oil, butter, honey, beaten eggs and buttermilk. Stir until mixed. Transfer to the baking tin and bake for 35 minutes.

Make the berry sauce. In a pan over a medium heat, place the strawberries, blueberries and raspberries. Add the sugar, lemon juice and lemon zest, and stir until the sugar has dissolved. Simmer for 3–4 minutes until the berries are cooked. Dissolve the cornflour in the 2 tablespoons water and add to the berries, stirring continuously until the sauce thickens. Simmer for 3 minutes, remove from the heat and leave to cool slightly. Serve warm.

Makes 6 servings

orange cranberry bread

see variations page 218

This lovely cranberry loaf, flavoured with orange, also has crunchy pecans and a gorgeous topping of sweet glaze.

170 g (6 oz) butter, room
    temperature + extra
    for greasing
170 g (6 oz) sugar
2 eggs, room temperature
120 ml (4 fl oz) orange juice
120 ml (4 fl oz) sour cream

1 tbsp orange zest
2 tsp vanilla extract
255 g (9 oz) plain flour
$\frac{1}{2}$ tsp salt
170 g (6 oz) dried cranberries
75 g (3 oz) chopped pecans

for glaze
100 g (4 oz) sieved icing
    sugar
3-4 tbsp orange liqueur
    (or orange juice)

Preheat the oven to 180°C (350°F) and grease a 450-g (1-lb) 20 x 10-cm (8 x 4-in) loaf tin with a little butter. In a large bowl, with an electric mixer, beat the butter and sugar together until pale and fluffy. Add the eggs, one at a time, beating well after each one. Add orange juice, sour cream, orange zest and vanilla, and beat until well blended. Fold in the flour, salt, cranberries and pecans until just combined. Transfer to the loaf tin, level the top and bake for about an hour, until a cocktail stick inserted into the centre comes out clean. Leave to cool in the tin for 5 minutes, and transfer to a wire rack to cool.

Make the glaze by mixing the icing sugar with enough orange liqueur to make a thick, syrup-like consistency, and drizzle it over the orange cranberry bread.

Makes 1 loaf

chocolate bread & butter dessert

see variations page 219

This is one of the easiest hot desserts to make, and a great way to use up stale bread.

10 large, thick slices day-old white bread
175 g (6 oz) good-quality dark chocolate
415 ml (14 fl oz) whipping cream
5 tbsp dark rum

100 g (4 oz) sugar
100 g (4 oz) unsalted butter + extra for greasing
1 tsp vanilla extract
3 eggs, room temperature

Generously butter a large shallow baking dish. Remove the crusts from the bread slices, and cut each slice into four triangles. Set a medium bowl over a pan of barely simmering water, ensuring the bowl does not touch the water. Place the chocolate, whipping cream, rum, sugar, butter and vanilla in the bowl, and heat it gently until the chocolate and butter have melted, and the sugar has dissolved. Remove the bowl from the heat and stir until smooth.

In another bowl, whisk the eggs with an electric mixer, add the chocolate mixture and whisk again until well combined. Spoon some of the mixture into the baking dish until it is about 1.5 cm ($\frac{1}{2}$ in) deep. Add half of the bread triangles, overlapping them in a single layer, and pour half of the remaining chocolate mixture evenly over the top. Arrange the remaining bread triangles as before, and pour over the rest of the chocolate mixture. Using the back of a spoon, press the bread triangles down into the chocolate so that they absorb some of the liquid. Cover with cling film, set aside for an hour until cold and chill in the fridge for 8–24 hours. Preheat the oven to 180°C (350°F). Remove the cover and bake for 30–35 minutes, until the top is crunchy and the centre is still soft. Remove from the oven and allow to stand for 10 minutes before serving.

Makes 6 servings

overnight caramel, peach & pecan french toast

see variations page 220

This is excellent as a dessert with whipped cream or ice cream and chocolate sauce, or serve for breakfast with maple syrup on the side. Best made with day-old bread.

170 g (6 oz) brown sugar
100 g (4 oz) butter
2 tbsp golden syrup
100 g (4 oz) chopped pecans
18 thick slices French bread

3 fresh ripe peaches, stoned
   and sliced
6 eggs, lightly beaten
355 ml (12 fl oz) whole milk
1 tsp vanilla extract

1 tbsp sugar
2 tsp cinnamon
$^1/_2$ tsp ground nutmeg
icing sugar, to serve

Make the caramel. In a medium pan, gently heat the brown sugar, butter and golden syrup together. Stir until the butter has melted and the sugar has dissolved. Pour into an ungreased 23 x 32-cm (9 x 13-in) baking dish, and sprinkle with half the pecans. Arrange half the bread slices in a single layer on top of the caramel, add the sliced peaches, sprinkle with the rest of the pecans and finish with the remaining bread slices in a single layer. In a medium bowl, whisk the eggs, milk and vanilla together, and carefully pour over the bread slices. In a small bowl, mix the sugar, cinnamon and nutmeg together, and sprinkle it over the bread. Cover with cling film and chill in the fridge for 8–24 hours.

Preheat the oven to 180°C (350°F). Remove the cover and bake for 30–40 minutes, until lightly browned. Leave to stand for 10 minutes. To serve, remove individual portions with a spatula and invert on to serving plates. Dust with icing sugar before serving.

Makes 9 servings

glazed fruit bread

see variations page 221

This would be great sliced and spread with butter for an after-school snack.

1 tsp sugar
160 ml (5 fl oz) warm water
2 tsp active dry yeast
450 g (1 lb) plain flour
1 tsp salt
1 tsp ground pumpkin pie spice
6 tbsp cold butter, diced + extra for greasing

75 g (3 oz) brown sugar
140 g (5 oz) currants
140 g (5 oz) raisins
140 g (5 oz) sultanas
140 g (5 oz) dried, stoned, chopped dates
1 egg, room temperature, lightly beaten
honey for glaze

Lightly butter two 450-g (1-lb) 20 x 10-cm (8 x 4-in) loaf tins. Dissolve the sugar in the warm water, sprinkle the yeast on top and leave for 10–15 minutes until frothy. In a large bowl, combine the flour, salt and pumpkin pie spice. Add the butter, and cut in until the mixture resembles fine breadcrumbs. Stir in the brown sugar and mixed dried fruits. Make a well in the centre, pour in the yeast liquid and the beaten egg and mix well until the dough leaves the sides of the bowl clean. Turn out on to a lightly floured work surface and knead for about 10 minutes, or until the dough is smooth and elastic. Place the dough in a large lightly oiled bowl, cover and leave in a warm place for an hour or so, until doubled in size. Turn the dough out on to a lightly floured work surface and knead for 1–2 minutes. Divide the dough in half and shape to fit the two loaf tins. Place them in oiled plastic bags, and set aside until the dough has risen above the top of the tins. Preheat the oven to 180°C (350°F). Remove the plastic bags and bake for 50–60 minutes. Remove from the oven and turn out on to a wire rack. To glaze, brush the loaves with honey.

Makes 2 loaves

gugelhupf

see variations page 222

Originally from Austria or Germany, this is an enriched yeast bread that is baked in a special ring tin. If you do not have a gugelhupf tin, a bundt tin can be substituted.

2 tbsp sliced almonds
1 tsp + 2 tbsp sugar, divided
2 tbsp warm water
2 tsp active dry yeast
190 g (6¾ oz) plain flour
½ tsp salt

50 g (2 oz) cold butter, diced + extra for greasing
1 egg, room temperature, lightly beaten
160 ml (5 fl oz) warm milk
85 g (3 oz) currants
1 tbsp lemon zest
icing sugar for dusting

Generously butter a 20-cm (8-in) gugelhupf tin and sprinkle the sliced almonds around the tin. Dissolve 1 teaspoon sugar in the warm water, sprinkle the yeast on top and leave in a warm place for 10–15 minutes, until frothy. In a large bowl, combine the flour and salt, add the butter and cut in until the mixture resembles fine breadcrumbs. Stir in the 2 tablespoons of sugar, make a well in the centre and add the yeast mixture, egg and warm milk. Beat well for 5 minutes to form a smooth batter. Beat in the currants and lemon zest, and pour the mixture into the tin. Cover with a damp cloth and leave to rise in a warm place until the dough reaches the top of the tin, or doubles in size. This will take 1 or 2 hours. Preheat the oven to 180°C (350°F). Remove the cover and bake for about 45 minutes, or until golden brown. Cool in the tin for 5 minutes, then turn out on to a wire rack to cool completely. Dust with sieved icing sugar and, for best results, serve the same day it is made.

Makes 1 gugelhupf

summer fruit dessert

see variations page 223

Serve chilled with a big dollop of whipped cream for happy people all round.

300 g (11 oz) raspberries
225 g (8 oz) blackberries
100 g (4 oz) redcurrants
400 g (14 oz) strawberries, hulled and quartered

150 g (6 oz) sugar
3 tbsp crème de cassis (or blackcurrant cordial)
6–8 slices day-old white bread, crusts removed
whipped cream to serve

Line a 1.2-l pudding basin with a double layer of cling film, leaving a good-size overlap around the top of the basin. When the dessert is finished, this will be brought up to cover the top. Wash and drain the fruit. In a large pan, place all the fruit, except the strawberries, with the sugar and crème de cassis. Heat gently for 3 minutes, until the juice starts to leak out of the fruit. Add the strawberries and cook for 2 minutes more. Set a sieve over a wide bowl and drain the juice from the fruit into the bowl.

To assemble the dessert, dip the slices of bread into the fruit juice, and use them to line the basin. Start with the bottom pieces, then lay soaked rectangles of bread along the sides of the basin, making sure there are no gaps between the slices, and reserving some for the top. Transfer the fruit to the bread-lined basin and pack it down. Finish with a layer of juice-soaked bread across the top, again making sure there are no gaps. Pour over any juice you have left and bring the overhanging cling film over the top. Place a small plate on the cling film covering, and place a weight on top. Chill in the fridge for 2–24 hours; overnight is best. To serve, peel away the cling film from the top. Place a serving plate over the top and invert the dessert on to the plate. Carefully peel away the cling film and serve in slices with cream.

Makes 6 servings

sweet swirl bread

see variations page 224

This cinnamon-crusted sweet bread is ideal to have with coffee halfway through the morning.

255 g (9 oz) plain flour
2 tbsp + 100 g (4 oz) sugar
$\frac{1}{2}$ tsp salt
2 tsp instant dry yeast
240 ml (8 fl oz) whole milk

3 tbsp white vegetable fat
130 g ($4\frac{1}{2}$ oz) white bread flour
oil for greasing
50 g (2 oz) mixed chopped nuts
2 tbsp brown sugar

1 tsp cinnamon
100 g (4 oz) butter, melted
50 g (2 oz) icing sugar
1–2 tsp whole milk

Grease one 30-cm (12-in) pizza tin or a large baking sheet. In the bowl of a stand mixer, combine 260 g (9 oz) plain flour with 2 tablespoons sugar. Add the salt on one side and the yeast on the other. In a small pan over a gentle heat, warm the milk and the white vegetable fat, until very warm. Make a well in the centre of the flour mixture and pour in the milk mixture. Using the dough hook attachment, blend at low speed until moistened. Beat for 3 minutes at medium speed. Add the bread flour and mix until the dough pulls away from the sides of the bowl. Knead the dough for 5–8 minutes, until smooth and elastic. Place dough in a large lightly oiled bowl, cover and put in a warm place for an hour or so, until doubled in size.

In a shallow dish or pie tin, combine nuts, 100 g (4 oz) sugar, brown sugar and cinnamon, and mix well. Place melted butter in another shallow dish or pie tin. Turn the dough out on to a lightly floured work surface, and punch down to remove the air bubbles. Pinch off a 5-cm (2-in) piece of dough, and roll into 6 x 1.5-cm ($\frac{1}{2}$-in) strips. Repeat with remaining dough. Dip each dough strip in butter to coat, then roll in sugar mixture to coat evenly. Place one strip in centre of tin and wind tightly to form a coil. Repeat with remaining strips,

placing close together to make a round, flat cake, ever increasing in size. Cover and leave
to rise in a warm place for an hour, until doubled in size. Preheat the oven to 180°C (350°F).
Uncover cake and bake for 20–25 minutes, or until golden brown. Cool for 5 minutes,
carefully remove from tin and transfer to plate. In a small bowl, combine the ingredients for
the glaze, adding enough milk to form a drizzling consistency. Drizzle over the coffee cake.

Makes 16 servings

praline, chocolate & cherry bread pudding

see variations page 225

This is a luscious and rich dessert, ideal for a special occasion.

240 ml (8 fl oz) whipping cream
4 tbsp Irish cream liqueur
2 tbsp sugar
1 tsp vanilla extract
1 tsp cornflour
2 tsp water
3 eggs, room temperature

65 g (2 1/2 oz) sugar
2 tsp vanilla extract
355 ml (12 fl oz) whipping
   cream, divided
80 ml (3 fl oz) whole milk
100 g (4 oz) dark
   chocolate, chopped

100 g (4 oz) praline-filled
   milk chocolate, chopped
   (such as Guylian)
1 large baguette, cubed
85 g (3 oz) glacé cherries
sugar for sprinkling
butter for greasing

In a medium pan over a medium heat, bring the cream, liqueur, sugar and vanilla to the boil. In a small bowl, mix the cornflour and water to a paste, and whisk into the cream mixture. Simmer gently for 3 minutes until thickened, stirring continuously. Remove from the heat, cool and transfer to a small bowl. Cover and refrigerate for at least 2 hours. In a large bowl, whisk together the eggs, sugar, vanilla, 240 ml (8 fl oz) cream and milk. Add the chocolate, bread and cherries, and stir to combine. Press the bread down so that it absorbs some of the liquid, and leave to stand for 30 minutes, stirring occasionally. Preheat the oven to 180°C (350°F) and grease six individual ramekin dishes with a little butter. Divide the bread mixture equally among the ramekin dishes and drizzle with the remaining cream. Sprinkle each with a little sugar and bake for 20 minutes, or until the custard is set. If the top looks like it is darkening too much, turn the oven down to 150°C (300°F) for the last 5–10 minutes. Allow to stand for 10 minutes and serve the dessert warm, with the sauce chilled.

Makes 6 servings

caribbean bread pudding

see base recipe page 199

pineapple, coconut & macadamia nut bread pudding
Prepare the basic recipe, adding 30 g (1 oz) chopped macadamia nuts with the coconut.

cherry, coconut & almond bread pudding
Prepare the basic recipe, replacing the pineapple with 30 g (1 oz) glacé cherries. Add 30 g (1 oz) sliced almonds with the coconut.

strawberry & white chocolate bread pudding
Prepare the basic recipe, replacing the pineapple with 50 g (2 oz) hulled and sliced strawberries. Add 75 g (3 oz) white chocolate chips with the coconut.

lemon & almond bread pudding
Prepare the basic recipe, replacing the pineapple with the zest of 2 lemons. Add 50 g (2 oz) sliced almonds with the coconut.

variations

chocolate marbled bread

see base recipe page 200

chocolate & pecan marbled bread
Prepare the basic recipe, adding 50 g (2 oz) chopped pecans to the chocolate batter.

white chocolate & strawberry marbled bread
Prepare the basic recipe, replacing the dark chocolate chips with white chocolate chips, and adding 2 teaspoons imitation strawberry extract and a few drops of red food colouring to turn the white chocolate batter pink.

chocolate-cardamom marbled bread
Prepare the basic recipe, adding 1 teaspoon crushed cardamom seeds to the chocolate batter.

dairy-free chocolate marbled bread
Prepare the basic recipe, replacing the butter and buttermilk with dairy-free margarine and whole coconut milk. Use chopped dairy-free dark chocolate if you can't find dairy-free chocolate chips.

sweet cornbread with summer berry sauce

see base recipe page 202

strawberry cornbread with summer berry sauce
Prepare the basic recipe, adding 100 g (4 oz) hulled and chopped strawberries, dried on kitchen paper, and 2 teaspoons imitation strawberry extract to the mixture.

chocolate chip cornbread with butterscotch sauce
Prepare the basic recipe, adding 150 g (5½ oz) chocolate chips to the mixture. Serve with butterscotch sauce (see Moravian sugar cake variation recipe page 279).

lemon cornbread with summer berry sauce
Prepare the basic recipe, adding the zest of 2 lemons to the mixture.

dairy-free cornbread with summer berry sauce
Prepare the basic recipe, replacing the butter and buttermilk with dairy-free margarine and whole coconut milk.

variations

orange cranberry bread

see base recipe page 203

lemon & almond bread

Prepare the basic recipe, omitting the orange juice, orange zest, cranberries and pecans.
Replace with 2 tablespoons lemon juice, 2 teaspoons lemon extract, 2 tablespoons lemon
zest, an extra 60 ml (2 fl oz) sour cream and 125 g (4½ oz) sliced almonds. Make a lemon
drizzle glaze by mixing 30 g (1 oz) sieved icing sugar with enough lemon juice to make a
runny icing. Drizzle over loaf.

orange cranberry bread with grand marnier glaze

Whisk together 3 tablespoons melted butter, 3 tablespoons Grand Marnier and 125 g (4½ oz)
sieved icing sugar. Add milk to thin to desired consistency, and spread over cooled bread.

butterscotch raisin bread

Prepare the basic recipe, replacing the cranberries and pecans with 170 g (6 oz) raisins and
100 g (4 oz) butterscotch chips.

white chocolate & cherry bread

Prepare the basic recipe, replacing the cranberries and pecans with 170 g (6 oz) dried cherries
and 100 g (4 oz) white chocolate chips.

variations

chocolate bread & butter dessert

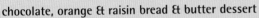

see base recipe page 205

chocolate, orange & raisin bread & butter dessert

Prepare the basic recipe, replacing the vanilla extract with 1 teaspoon pure orange extract. Scatter 50 g (2 oz) raisins over the first layer of bread triangles.

mocha pecan bread & butter dessert

Prepare the basic recipe, replacing the vanilla extract with 2 teaspoons instant coffee powder mixed with 2 teaspoons boiling water.

chocolate-butterscotch bread & butter dessert

Prepare the basic recipe. Sprinkle 75 g (3 oz) butterscotch chips over the first layer of bread triangles.

chocolate-amaretto bread pudding

Prepare the basic recipe, replacing the vanilla extract with 1 tablespoon amaretto. Scatter 30 g (1 oz) broken amaretti cookies over the first layer of bread triangles.

variations

overnight caramel, peach & pecan french toast

see base recipe page 206

overnight caramel, banana & coconut french toast
Prepare the basic recipe, replacing the peaches and pecans with 2 sliced bananas and 75 g (3 oz) sweetened coconut flakes.

overnight caramel, strawberry & almond french toast
Prepare the basic recipe, replacing the peaches and pecans with 100 g (4 oz) hulled and sliced fresh strawberries and 60 g (2 oz) sliced almonds. Scatter 40 g (1½ oz) sliced almonds over the top just before baking.

overnight caramel-pecan, peanut butter & chocolate french toast
Prepare the basic recipe, replacing the peaches with 75 g (3 oz) peanut butter chips and 75 g (3 oz) dark chocolate chips.

overnight caramel, blueberry & walnut french toast
Prepare the basic recipe, replacing the peaches with 100 g (4 oz) fresh blueberries.

glazed fruit bread

see base recipe page 207

sweet potato & fruit bread french toast with cinnamon butter
Prepare the basic recipe, and cut the loaf into slices. Make batter by mixing together 1 egg, 125 g (4½ oz) plain flour, 1 tablespoon brown sugar, 2 tablespoons vegetable oil, 3 teaspoons baking powder, ½ teaspoon salt and 100 g (4 oz) sweet potato purée. Dip slices of fruit bread in the batter and fry for a few minutes each side. Serve with maple syrup and cinnamon butter: 100 g (4 oz) softened butter mixed with 1 teaspoon cinnamon.

glazed fruit bread with cherries & brandy
Prepare the basic recipe, replacing the currants and raisins with 140 g (5 oz) dried cherries and 140 g (5 oz) glacé cherries. Add 2 tablespoons brandy to the mixture with the beaten egg. If this makes the mixture too sticky, add just a little more flour.

glazed fruit bread with apples & cinnamon
Prepare the basic recipe, replacing the currants with 1 peeled, cored and chopped apple, and adding 1 teaspoon cinnamon.

glazed fruit bread with fresh blueberries
Prepare the basic recipe, replacing the sultanas with 100 g (4 oz) fresh blueberries.

variations

gugelhupf

see base recipe page 208

lemon-glazed mixed fruit gugelhupf
Prepare the basic recipe, omitting the almonds in the bottom of the tin and the dusting of icing sugar, and adding 30 g (1 oz) each chopped dried cherries and apricots. Make a glaze with 30 g (1 oz) sieved icing sugar with enough freshly squeezed lemon juice to make a runny icing. Drizzle it over the cold gugelhupf.

orange, cherry & walnut gugelhupf
Prepare the basic recipe, replacing the currants and lemon zest with dried cherries and the zest of 1 orange.

apricot & almond gugelhupf
Prepare the basic recipe, replacing the currants with 85 g (3 oz) chopped dried ready-to-eat apricots.

date & pecan gugelhupf
Prepare the basic recipe, replacing the currants and almonds with chopped, dried ready-to-eat dates and chopped pecans.

variations

summer fruit dessert

see base recipe page 211

french toast with summer fruit
Prepare the fruit. Cut 8 thick slices of bread in half. Mix a batter with 2 eggs, 2 egg whites,
6 tablespoons milk, 7 tablespoons apple juice, 50 g (2 oz) sugar and a pinch of salt. Heat a
little butter in a large frying pan and fry soaked bread slices on both sides for a few minutes,
until golden brown. Dust with icing sugar and serve topped with the fruit.

peach & plum fruit dessert
Prepare the basic recipe. Omit the redcurrants and blackberries, and substitute 200 g (7 oz)
stoned and chopped plums and 100 g (4 oz) stoned and chopped peaches. Cook the plums
and peaches first for 5 minutes, then proceed as directed.

apple, rhubarb & orange fruit dessert
Prepare the basic recipe, replacing the redcurrants and blackberries with 200 g (7 oz) peeled,
cored and chopped apples, and adding 100 g (4 oz) chopped rhubarb with the zest of
1 orange. Cook the apples and rhubarb first for 5 minutes, then proceed as directed.

summer fruit dessert with mascarpone cream
Prepare the basic recipe and serve with one 225-g (8-oz) tub mascarpone mixed with
3 tablespoons double cream, 3 tablespoons honey and the seeds scraped from a vanilla pod.
Stir until smooth and chill until needed.

variations

sweet swirl bread

see base recipe page 212

chocolate chip swirl bread
Prepare the basic recipe, replacing the nuts with 75 g (3 oz) dark chocolate chips.

peanut butter & pecan swirl bread
Prepare the basic recipe, replacing the nuts with 50 g (2 oz) peanut butter chips and 40 g
(1½ oz) chopped pecans.

apple & cinnamon pull-apart bread
Prepare the basic recipe. Add 1 peeled, cored and chopped apple to the nuts and sugar.
Press the dough into a 50 x 30-cm (20 x 12-in) rectangle, brush with 60 g (2 oz) melted
butter and sprinkle with the filling. Slice the dough vertically into 6 equal strips of 10 x
30 cm (4 x 12 in), stack the strips on top of each other and slice the stack into 6 equal slices,
giving 6 stacks of 6 squares. Layer the squares into a greased 900-g (2-lb) loaf tin, cover and
leave for 45 minutes. Bake for 35–40 minutes. Cool in tin, invert on to a plate and glaze with
170 g (6 oz) icing sugar mixed with 3 tablespoons milk.

orange & lemon pull-apart bread
Prepare the basic recipe, using the method for apple and cinnamon pull-apart bread. Omit
the filling and use 200 g (7 oz) sugar and the zest of 4 lemons and 1 orange. Brush the
dough with 60 g (2 oz) melted butter and proceed as above. Replace the milk in the glaze
with lemon juice.

praline, chocolate & cherry bread pudding

see base recipe page 214

praline, white chocolate & blueberry bread pudding
Prepare the basic recipe, replacing the dark chocolate and glacé cherries with good-quality white chocolate and 50 g (2 oz) fresh blueberries.

caramel, chocolate & raisin challah pudding
Prepare the basic recipe, replacing the praline-filled chocolates with caramel-filled chocolates, and the cherries and French bread with raisins and challah.

praline, pecan & peach bread pudding
Prepare the basic recipe, replacing the cherries with 2 fresh stoned and chopped peaches, and adding 40 g (1½ oz) chopped pecans to the mixture.

praline, chocolate & amaretto bread pudding
Prepare the basic recipe, replacing 2 tablespoons milk with amaretto liqueur.

rolls, scones
& bagels

In this chapter, you will find inspiration for making
your own scones or hamburger buns from scratch,
rolls to accompany dinner and the best cinnamon
buns you have ever tasted.

yeasted buttermilk scones

see variations page 246

For best results, the dough for these yummy scones should be chilled overnight.

1 tsp + 3 tbsp sugar, divided
160 ml (5 fl oz) warm water
1 tbsp instant dry yeast
640 g (1 lb 6½ oz) plain flour
5 tsp baking powder

½ tsp bicarbonate of soda
1 tsp salt
240 ml (8 fl oz) sunflower oil
475 ml (16 fl oz) buttermilk

Dissolve 1 teaspoon sugar in the warm water, sprinkle the yeast on top and leave for 10–15 minutes until frothy. In the bowl of a stand mixer, combine the flour, baking powder, bicarbonate of soda, 3 tablespoons sugar and salt. Make a well in the centre, and add the yeast liquid, oil and buttermilk. With a dough hook attachment, mix until a dough starts to come together. Knead on medium speed for 5–8 minutes, until the dough is smooth and elastic. Transfer the dough to a large lightly oiled bowl and turn to coat it all over. Cover and leave in the fridge for 8–24 hours.

Line four large baking sheets with baking paper. Turn the dough out on to a floured work surface and gently deflate the dough. Divide it in half, place one half back in the bowl and keep covered. Lightly roll one half out to about 1.5 cm (½ in) thick. Cut out scones with a floured 6-cm (2½-in) cutter and place them on the baking sheets, barely touching. Loosely cover with cling film and leave in a warm place for 20–30 minutes, until slightly risen and puffy. Repeat with the other half of the dough. Preheat the oven to 200°C (400°F). Remove cling film and bake the scones for 10–15 minutes, or until lightly browned. Cool on a rack.

Makes 48 scones

beer bread rolls

see variations page 247

Use a good-quality, dark and full-flavoured beer, to produce a complex, nutty flavour.

1 tsp sugar
55 ml (2 fl oz) warm water
2 tsp active dry yeast
450 g (1 lb) white bread flour

300 g (10½ oz) rolled oats,
   ground fine
25 g (1 oz) wheat germ
½ tsp salt

350 ml (12½ fl oz) brown ale
25 ml (1 fl oz) maple syrup
2 tbsp olive oil
1 egg + 1 egg white, room
   temperature, lightly beaten

Line 2 large baking sheets with baking paper. Dissolve the sugar in the warm water, sprinkle the yeast on top, and leave for 10–15 minutes until frothy. In a large bowl, combine the flour, ground oats, wheat germ and salt. Make a well in the centre and pour in the yeast liquid, brown ale, maple syrup, olive oil and the whole egg. Mix until a soft dough comes together. Turn out onto a lightly floured work surface and knead for 10 minutes, until the dough is smooth and elastic. Alternatively, knead in an electric mixer with a dough hook attachment for 5–8 minutes. Place the dough in a large lightly oiled bowl and turn to coat it all over. Cover and leave in a warm place for an hour or so, until doubled in size.

Turn out onto a lightly floured work surface and divide into 12–16 equal portions, depending upon the size of the rolls that you require. Form each piece into a ball, tucking the dough underneath and pinching together. Place the rolls on the lined baking sheets, seam underneath, and cover with lightly oiled cling film. Leave to rise again for another hour, or until doubled in size. Preheat the oven to 180°C (375°F). Remove cover, brush with the beaten egg white and bake for 25–30 minutes, or until golden brown. Cool on a wire rack.

Makes 12–16 rolls

english muffins

see variations page 248

These muffins have a crisper crust than the shop-bought kind, and a much fresher taste.

3 tbsp polenta
1 tsp sugar, dissolved in 60 ml (2 fl oz) warm water
2 tsp active dry yeast

450 g (1 lb) white bread flour
1 tsp salt
2 tbsp olive oil

Line two large baking sheets with baking paper and generously sprinkle with polenta. Sprinkle the yeast on top of the sugar–water mix, and leave for 10–15 minutes until frothy. In the bowl of a stand mixer fitted with a dough hook attachment, combine the flour and salt. Make a well in the centre, and add the yeast liquid and the olive oil. Mix to a soft dough. Knead for 5–8 minutes, until the dough feels soft, smooth and elastic. Transfer the dough to a large lightly oiled bowl and turn to coat it all over. Cover and leave in a warm place for an hour or so, or until doubled in size. Turn the dough out on to a lightly floured work surface and punch down. Knead for 2 minutes and divide in half. Leave to rest for 5 minutes. Roll out one half of the dough until it is 6 mm (¼ in) thick, and cut out rounds with a 7.5-cm (3-in) cutter. Place the rounds on the lined baking sheet, and turn each one to coat each side with polenta. Repeat with the other half of the dough. Cover with cling film and leave in a warm place for 45 minutes.

If you have a griddle, grease it with a trace of oil and heat it until it is moderately hot. Cook the muffins until the bottoms are nicely browned, turn, and cook the other side. Cooking times will vary according to the temperature of your oven, but should take 6–10 minutes each side. Cool on a wire rack.

Makes 14 muffins

traditional dinner rolls

see variations page 249

There is nothing better than fresh-from-the-oven, heavenly warm rolls to mop up all the yummy sauce at dinner.

2 tsp sugar
445 ml (15 fl oz) + 2 tbsp warm water
2 tsp active dry yeast

640 g (1^1/$_2$ lb) white bread flour
2 tsp salt
2 tbsp unsalted butter, softened

Line two large baking sheets with baking paper.

Dissolve the sugar in the warm water, sprinkle the yeast on top and leave for 10–15 minutes until frothy. In a large bowl, mix the flour and salt together, make a well in the centre and pour in the yeast liquid and the softened butter. Mix to a soft dough. If the dough feels too dry, add a little more water, and if it feels too sticky, add a little more flour. Turn out on to a lightly floured work surface and knead for 10 minutes until the dough is smooth and elastic. Transfer to a large lightly oiled bowl and turn to coat it all over. Cover and put in a warm place for an hour or so, or until doubled in size.

Turn the dough out on to a lightly floured work surface and divide into 18 equal portions. Roll each piece into a ball, turning the edges of the dough under, and pinching the dough together underneath. Place the rolls on the baking sheets, cover with cling film and leave to rise again for 30–40 minutes at room temperature. Preheat the oven to 230°C (450°F). Remove covers and bake the rolls for 15–20 minutes. Cool on a wire rack.

Makes 18 rolls

onion bagels

see variations page 250

Easier to make than you might think, bagels are superb filled with, well, just about anything.

1 tbsp + 2 tbsp sugar, divided	450 g (1 lb) white bread flour	200 ml (7 fl oz) + 2 tbsp water
7 tbsp warm water	2 tsp onion salt	1 egg white, lightly beaten
2 tsp active dry yeast	2 tbsp dried onion flakes	onion seeds to sprinkle

Line two large baking sheets with baking paper. Dissolve 1 tablespoon sugar in the warm water, sprinkle the yeast on top and leave for 10–15 minutes until frothy. In a large bowl, combine the flour, salt and onion flakes. Make a well in the centre, pour in the yeast liquid and the cool water and mix to a soft dough. Turn the dough out on to a lightly floured work surface and knead for 10 minutes, until it feels smooth and elastic. Transfer to a large lightly oiled bowl and turn to coat it all over. Cover and put in a warm place for an hour or so, until doubled in size. Turn the dough out on to a lightly floured work surface and gently knock back. Divide into 10 equal portions, and shape each piece into a flat ball. Insert the handle of a wooden spoon in the centre to make a hole, and twirl the bagel around the handle to increase the size of the hole to about 3 cm (1$\frac{1}{4}$ in) wide. Repeat with the rest of the dough.

Preheat the oven to 200°C (400°F). Bring a large saucepan of water to a boil and add 2 tablespoons sugar. Gently slip two or three bagels at a time into the boiling water. Let them cook for 1 minute, turn them over and cook another 3 minutes. Remove with a slotted spoon, allowing them to drain over the water as you do so. Place them on the lined baking sheets, brush with a little egg white and sprinkle with onion seeds. Bake for 20–25 minutes, until golden brown and the bases sound hollow when tapped. Cool on a wire rack.

Makes 10 bagels

hamburger buns

see variations page 251

This book would not be complete without a recipe for hamburger buns, but they had to have a twist: garlic and Parmesan.

255 g (9 oz) plain flour
190 g (6¾ oz) white bread flour
2 tbsp sugar
1 tsp salt
1 tbsp instant dry yeast

180 ml (6 fl oz) warm water
4 tbsp butter
2 cloves garlic, minced
1 egg, room temperature, lightly beaten
2 tbsp grated Parmesan cheese

Line two large baking sheets with baking paper. In the bowl of a stand mixer fitted with a dough hook attachment, combine the flours and sugar. Add the salt on one side and the yeast on the other. Make a well in the centre and add the warm water, half the butter, garlic and egg. On a low speed, mix until a soft dough forms. Knead on medium speed for 5–8 minutes until the dough is smooth and elastic. Transfer to a large lightly oiled bowl and turn to coat it all over. Cover and put in a warm place for an hour or so, until doubled in size.

Turn out on to a lightly floured work surface and gently deflate the dough. Divide into 12 equal portions and shape each piece into a round ball. Flatten each one to about 7.5 cm (3 in) in diameter. Place the buns on the baking sheets, cover and leave in a warm place for an hour or so, until puffy. Melt the remaining butter, brush a little over the top of each bun, and bake for 15–18 minutes, until golden brown. Remove from the oven and brush with more melted butter, and sprinkle with a little Parmesan cheese. Cool on a wire rack.

Makes 12 buns

cinnamon buns with soft icing

see variations page 252

These buns have a subtle tang of lemon in the pastry dough, which contrasts beautifully with the sweetness of the thick glaze.

1 tsp + 4 tbsp sugar, divided
120 ml (4 fl oz) warm milk
2 tsp active dry yeast
285 g (10 oz) white bread flour
½ tsp salt
½ tsp bicarbonate of soda
1 egg, room temperature

1 tsp vanilla extract
zest of 1 lemon
2 tbsp sour cream
2 tbsp butter + extra for
    greasing and brushing
40 g (1½ oz) dark brown sugar
1 tsp cinnamon

for the icing
100 g (4 oz) icing sugar,
    sieved
2–3 tbsp milk
½ tsp glycerin (optional)

Grease a 20-cm (8-in) square cake tin with a little butter. Dissolve 1 teaspoon sugar in the warm milk, sprinkle the yeast on top, and leave for 10–15 minutes until frothy. In a large bowl, combine the flour, salt, bicarbonate of soda and 4 tablespoons sugar. In a small bowl, whisk the egg, vanilla, lemon zest and sour cream together. Make a well in the centre of the flour, and add the egg and sour cream with the yeast liquid. Work to a soft dough, adding a little more milk if the dough feels too dry, and a little more flour if it feels too sticky. Turn out on to a lightly floured surface and knead until you have a soft, smooth and elastic dough. Alternatively, knead the dough in a stand mixer with a dough hook attachment for 5–8 minutes. Place dough in a large lightly oiled bowl and turn it around so that it is coated all over. Cover and leave in a warm place for an hour or so, or until doubled in size.

In a medium bowl, combine the butter with the brown sugar and cinnamon. When the dough has doubled in size, turn it out on to a lightly floured surface, punch down, knead lightly and roll out to a 30 x 15-cm (12 x 6-in) rectangle. Spread the butter and sugar

mixture evenly over the surface, leaving a small margin around the edges. Roll tightly into a cylinder, sealing the far edge. Turn the cylinder so that the seam is underneath, and cut into nine equal slices. Arrange the slices, touching, in the cake tin. Cover and leave to rise in a warm place for about 30 minutes. Preheat the oven to 180°C (350°F). Brush with a little melted butter and bake for 30 minutes, until golden brown. Leave to cool in the tin for 5 minutes, then transfer to a wire rack, placing them close together. In a small bowl, beat the icing sugar and just enough milk to make a smooth icing. Spread over the buns while they are warm, allowing a little to run down the edges. Best served immediately.

Makes 9 buns

sweet braided rolls

see variations page 253

These impressive-looking rolls are quite sweet, which makes them excellent with morning coffee.

170 g (6 oz) unsalted butter
205 ml (7 fl oz) + 2 tbsp whole milk
510 g (1 lb 2 oz) plain flour
2 tbsp sugar

2 tsp instant dry yeast
pinch of salt
2 eggs, room temperature, lightly beaten
3 tbsp icing sugar

In a medium pan, gently heat the butter and milk together until the butter has melted. Cool until lukewarm. Place the flour in the bowl of a stand mixer with a dough hook attachment, and stir in the sugar. Put the yeast on one side and the pinch of salt on the other. Make a well in the centre, and pour in the milk and butter and the eggs. Mix until a dough starts to form. Knead for 5 minutes. Transfer to a large lightly oiled bowl, cover and leave in a warm place for 30 minutes.

Line two large baking sheets with baking paper. Turn the dough out on to a lightly floured work surface and divide into 24 equal portions. Roll each piece into a small log and roll in the icing sugar. Lay three pieces of dough side by side, and pinch the pieces of dough together at one end. Braid the roll from that end and pinch the other ends together to complete the roll. Repeat with the rest of the dough. Lay the completed rolls on the baking sheets, cover with cling film and leave to rise again for 30 minutes. Preheat the oven to 170°C (325°F). Remove the cling film and bake the rolls for 20 minutes, or until light golden in colour. Cool on a wire rack.

Makes 8 rolls

lancashire barm cakes

see variations page 254

These are sometimes called soft baps, and are wonderful filled with crispy bacon and ketchup, and seasoned with plenty of ground white pepper.

1 tsp sugar
300 ml (10 fl oz) warm milk and water mixed
(roughly half of each)
2 tsp active dry yeast

450 g (1 lb) white bread flour +
extra for dredging
1 tsp salt
50 g (2 oz) white vegetable fat

Line two large baking sheets with baking paper. Dissolve the sugar in the warm milk and water, sprinkle the yeast on top and leave for 10–15 minutes until frothy. In a large bowl, combine the flour and salt, and cut in the white vegetable fat until the mixture resembles fine breadcrumbs. Make a well in the centre and pour in the yeast liquid. Mix until a soft dough forms, and turn out on to a lightly floured work surface and knead for 10 minutes, using your hands and knuckles. Alternatively, knead in an electric mixer with a dough hook attachment for 5–8 minutes. Transfer the dough to a large lightly oiled bowl and turn to coat it all over. Cover and leave in a warm place for an hour or so, or until doubled in size.

Turn the dough out on to a lightly floured work surface and carefully deflate the dough. Knead gently for 2 minutes to make a firm dough and divide into 10 equal portions. Shape each one into a ball and roll out to a circle about 1.5 cm (½ in) thick. Place on the baking sheets and dredge the tops with flour. Cover with cling film and leave to rise again for about 30 minutes at room temperature. Preheat the oven to 200°C (400°F). Remove cling film and bake the barm cakes for 15–20 minutes, or until golden brown. Cool on a rack.

Makes 10 cakes

soft wholewheat pull-apart rolls

see variations page 255

These delicious soft rolls are baked in a muffin pan, three little balls together, which look very attractive when baked.

2 tsp + 55 g (2 oz) sugar, divided
175 ml (6 fl oz) warm water
4 tsp active dry yeast
300 g (1 lb 5 oz) white bread flour

185 g (6½ oz) wholewheat flour
1 tsp salt
240 ml (8 fl oz) whole milk
25 g (1 oz) butter, softened + extra for greasing

Grease a 12-cup muffin pan with butter. Dissolve 2 teaspoons sugar in the warm water, sprinkle the yeast on top and leave for 10–15 minutes until frothy. In the bowl of a stand mixer with a dough hook attachment, combine the flours, salt and the remaining sugar. Make a well in the centre, and add the yeast liquid, milk and softened butter. Mix to a soft dough. The dough will feel quite wet, but if it seems too sticky, add a little more flour. Knead for 5–8 minutes, until the dough is smooth and elastic. Transfer to a large lightly oiled bowl and turn to coat it all over. Cover and put in a warm place for an hour or so, or until doubled in size.

Preheat the oven to 180°C (350°F). Turn the dough out onto a lightly floured work surface and gently deflate the dough. Pull off pieces of dough big enough to form into 2.5-cm (1-in) balls, and insert three at a time into each muffin cup. It will be a tight fit. Dust with flour and cover with cling film. Leave at room temperature for 30 minutes, until well risen. Remove the cling film and bake the rolls for 25–30 minutes, or until light golden in colour. Remove from the oven and brush with a little butter. Cool on a wire rack.

Makes 12 rolls

honey wheat rolls

see variations page 256

These rolls are soft and delicious. Try rising them overnight in the fridge.

1 tsp sugar, dissolved in 240 ml (8 fl oz) water	385 g (13½ oz) wholewheat flour	60 ml (2 fl oz) orange juice
2 tsp active dry yeast	60 ml (2 fl oz) potato starch	50 g (2 oz) unsalted butter, diced
	1¼ tsp salt	3 tbsp honey

Line two large baking sheets with baking paper. Sprinkle the yeast on top of the sugar–water mix, and leave for 10–15 minutes until frothy. In a large bowl, whisk the flour, potato starch and salt together. Make a well in the centre, and add the yeast liquid, orange juice, butter and honey. Mix until a dough starts to come together. Turn out on to a lightly floured work surface, and knead using your hands and knuckles for about 10 minutes, until the dough feels soft, smooth and elastic. Alternatively, knead in an electric mixer with a dough hook attachment for 5–8 minutes. Place the dough in a large lightly oiled bowl and turn to coat it all over. Cover and leave at room temperature until quite puffy, and not quite doubled in size. This may take 2–3 hours.

Turn the dough out on to a lightly oiled work surface and gently deflate the dough. Divide into 24 equal portions. Roll each piece into a ball by tucking the dough underneath and pinching together, pressing down with the palm of your hand quite hard and then easing up. Place the rolls on the baking sheets, spacing them evenly, about 2.5 cm (1 in) apart. Cover the baking sheets with lightly oiled cling film and leave to rise again at room temperature for 1½–2 hours. Preheat the oven to 200°C (400°F). Remove the cling film and bake for 15–20 minutes, until golden brown. Cool on a wire rack.

Makes 24 rolls

quick gluten-free & yeast-free rolls

see variations page 257

These are the rolls to turn to if you cannot eat wheat, gluten, dairy, yeast, soy or eggs. They are surprisingly tasty and satisfying.

40 g (1½ oz) potato starch
75 g (3 oz) tapioca flour
65 g (2¼ oz) gram flour
2 tsp xanthan gum
1 tsp gluten-free baking powder
½ tsp salt

1 tbsp ground flaxseed
80 ml (3 fl oz) olive oil
210 ml (7 fl oz) chilled sparkling water
2 tsp ground flaxseed soaked for 5 minutes
   in 3 tbsp boiling water

Line a large baking sheet with baking paper. Preheat the oven to 200°C (400°F). In a large bowl, whisk the potato starch, tapioca flour, gram flour, xanthan gum, baking powder, salt and ground flaxseed together. Make a well in the centre, add the oil and stir together with a fork. Add the sparkling water and soaked flaxseed, stirring continuously, until you have a thick and sticky dough.

Spoon the dough on to the baking sheet, forming and moulding it into five or six rolls, depending on the size of the rolls you require. Bake for 20–25 minutes, until they have risen and are lightly coloured. Cool on a wire rack. Either freeze immediately or eat the same day.

Makes 5–6 rolls

variations

yeasted buttermilk scones

see base recipe page 227

rosemary yeasted buttermilk scones
Prepare the basic recipe, adding 2 teaspoons chopped fresh rosemary leaves to the flour.

cinnamon & raisin yeasted buttermilk scones
Prepare the basic recipe, adding 1 teaspoon cinnamon and 60 g (2 oz) raisins to the flour.

buttermilk scones with no yeast
Preheat oven to 220°C (425°F). Line a baking sheet with baking paper. In a medium bowl, mix together 250 g (9 oz) plain flour, 2 teaspoons baking powder, ½ teaspoon bicarbonate of soda and ½ teaspoon salt. Cut in 100 g (4 oz) diced unsalted butter until mixture resembles coarse breadcrumbs. Add 180 ml (6 fl oz) very cold buttermilk and stir until the dough comes together in a ball. On a lightly floured surface, knead the dough gently six times. Pat dough into a 25-cm (10-in) circle about 1.5 cm (½ in) thick. Cut dough into eight 7.5-cm (3-in) rounds with a lightly floured cutter. Place on the baking sheet about 5 cm (2 in) apart. Brush with buttermilk and bake for 12–15 minutes.

cheddar scones
Follow the recipe above and add 120 g (4½ oz) grated cheddar cheese and ¼ teaspoon garlic powder to the flour. Do not roll out. Drop 4-tbsp portions of dough on to the lined baking sheet and bake for 11–13 minutes at 200°C (400°F). Brush each scone with melted butter, and sprinkle with a little garlic salt and dried parsley.

beer bread rolls

see base recipe page 228

mixed seed & pecan rolls
Prepare the basic recipe, adding 2 tablespoons each of sesame seeds, poppy seeds, onion seeds, sunflower seeds and chopped pecans to the flour with the yeast liquid.

garlic & parsley beer bread rolls
Prepare the basic recipe, adding 2 minced cloves of garlic and 2 tablespoons chopped parsley to the flour with the yeast liquid.

sundried-tomato & olive beer bread rolls
Prepare the basic recipe, adding 25 g (1 oz) finely chopped sundried tomatoes and 2 tablespoons pitted and finely chopped black olives to the flour with the yeast liquid.

variations

english muffins

see base recipe page 231

cheese-topped english muffins
Prepare the basic recipe, adding 2 teaspoons grated cheddar cheese to the top of each muffin just before baking.

garlic & thyme english muffins
Prepare the basic recipe, adding 2 crushed cloves of garlic and 1 tablespoon dried thyme to the flour with the olive oil.

sundried-tomato english muffins
Prepare the basic recipe, adding 30 g (1 oz) finely chopped sundried tomatoes to the flour with the olive oil.

sweetened orange-scented english muffins
Prepare the basic recipe, adding the zest of 1 orange and 1 tablespoon sugar to the flour with the olive oil.

variations

traditional dinner rolls

see base recipe page 232

crusty dinner rolls
Prepare the basic recipe. When you turn on the oven, put a large roasting tin in to heat up. When the oven is hot, just before you bake the rolls, pour 750 ml (1½ pints) hot water into the hot roasting tin; this will create the steam that makes the rolls crusty. When the rolls are ready to bake, spray quickly with water, and put them straight into the oven. Bake as directed.

soft dinner rolls made with milk
Prepare the basic recipe, replacing 240 ml (8 fl oz) warm water with 240 ml (8 fl oz) warm milk. While the rolls are still hot, brush them with a little melted butter.

rosemary & thyme dinner rolls
Prepare the basic recipe, adding 2 teaspoons each of dried rosemary and thyme to the flour.

lemon & poppy-seed dinner rolls
Prepare the basic recipe, adding the zest of 1 lemon and 2 tablespoons poppy seeds to the flour. Just before baking, brush the rolls with beaten egg and sprinkle with poppy seeds.

variations

onion bagels

see base recipe page 233

cinnamon & raisin bagels
Prepare the basic recipe, omitting the onion salt, flakes and seeds. Add 1 tablespoon cinnamon, 225 g (8 oz) raisins and 1 tablespoon brown sugar to the flour with the yeast liquid.

cheese & chipotle chilli bagels
Prepare the basic recipe, omitting the onion salt, flakes and seeds. Add 1 teaspoon cayenne pepper, 2 teaspoons dried oregano, 85 g (3 oz) grated cheddar cheese and 2 finely chopped chipotle chillies. Brush the bagels with a little beaten egg just before baking and sprinkle with a little oregano.

baked egg bialys
Prepare the basic recipe, omitting the onion salt, flakes and seeds. After the first rising, punch down and cut the dough into 8 equal portions. Form into round rolls, place on the baking sheets, cover and leave to rise again. Pick up each roll and, holding it like a steering wheel, turn it around in your hands, making a large impression in the middle, big enough to hold a small egg. Put them back on the baking sheets and prick the indentations to stop them from rising. Brush the edges with beaten egg and break a small egg into the middle of each roll. Bake for 5 minutes at 220°C (425°F), and 10 minutes at 180°C (350°F).

blueberry & vanilla bagels
Prepare the basic recipe, omitting the onion salt, flakes and seeds. Add 1 tablespoon honey, 170 g (6 oz) dried blueberries and seeds of a vanilla pod to the flour with the yeast liquid.

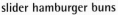

variations

hamburger buns

see base recipe page 234

slider hamburger buns
Prepare the basic recipe, replacing 120 ml (4 fl oz) warm water with 120 ml (4 fl oz) warm milk and the butter with white vegetable fat. Omit the garlic and make 18–20 hamburger buns instead of 12. Bake for 15–17 minutes.

hot dog buns
Prepare the basic recipe, but for hot dog buns, shape the balls into 12-cm (4½-in)-long cylinders. Flatten the cylinders slightly; dough rises more in the centre, so this will give a gently rounded top rather than a high top. Sprinkle with Parmesan cheese as directed.

sesame seed hamburger buns
Prepare the basic recipe, omitting the garlic and replacing the Parmesan cheese with sesame seeds.

poppy-seed hot dog buns
Prepare the basic hot dog recipe as above, omitting the garlic and replacing the Parmesan cheese with poppy seeds.

cinnamon buns with soft icing

see base recipe page 236

chocolate chip buns with chocolate icing
Prepare the basic recipe, omitting the lemon zest. Sprinkle on 50 g (2 oz) milk chocolate chips with the butter and sugar filling, and bake as directed. For the icing, replace 2 tablespoons icing sugar with sieved unsweetened cocoa powder.

apricot & almond cinnamon buns
Prepare the basic recipe and sprinkle on 50 g (2 oz) chopped, dried ready-to-eat apricots and 30 g (1 oz) sliced almonds with the butter and sugar filling.

cranberry & orange buns
Prepare the basic recipe, replacing the lemon zest with orange zest. Sprinkle on 85 g (3 oz) dried cranberries and another 2 teaspoons orange zest with the butter and sugar filling.

date & walnut cinnamon buns
Prepare the basic recipe, sprinkling on 50 g (2 oz) chopped, dried ready-to-eat dates and 30 g (1 oz) chopped walnuts with the butter and sugar filling.

variations

sweet braided rolls

see base recipe page 239

sugar-crusted sweet braided rolls

Prepare the basic recipe. When the rolls have cooled, brush each one with a little melted butter, and sprinkle with coarse sugar mixed with a little cinnamon.

sweet apricot & almond braided rolls

Prepare the basic recipe, adding 50 g (2 oz) chopped, dried ready-to-eat apricots and 30 g (1 oz) to the flour. Add a little water if the dough seems too dry. Brush the cooled rolls with a little melted butter and sprinkle with toasted sliced almonds.

maple pecan butter

Prepare the basic recipe, and serve with maple pecan butter. With an electric mixer, beat 100 g (4 oz) softened butter with 1 tablespoon maple syrup and 100 g (4 oz) toasted and finely chopped pecans. Chill.

sweet raisin braided rolls

Prepare the basic recipe, adding 50 g (2 oz) raisins to the flour.

variations

lancashire barm cakes

see base recipe page 240

onion-seed floured baps
Prepare the basic recipe, adding 2 tablespoons onion seeds to the flour. Roll the balls into slight ovals rather than circles and generously dredge each one with flour. Bake as directed.

olive & basil barm cakes
Prepare the basic recipe, adding 40 g (1½ oz) pitted and finely chopped black olives and 3 tablespoons freshly chopped basil to the flour with the yeast liquid.

apple & blue cheese barm cakes
Prepare the basic recipe, adding 1 peeled, cored and finely chopped apple and 40 g (1½ oz) crumbled blue cheese to the flour with the yeast liquid.

variations

soft wholewheat pull-apart rolls

see base recipe page 242

soft olive wholewheat pull-apart rolls
Prepare the basic recipe, adding 85 g (3 oz) chopped pitted black olives to the flour with the softened butter.

soft caraway-seed wholewheat pull-apart rolls
Prepare the basic recipe, adding 4 tablespoons caraway seeds to the flour.

soft oat-topped poppy seed pull-apart rolls
Prepare the basic recipe, adding 4 tablespoons poppy seeds to the flour. Just before baking, brush the rolls with a little melted butter and sprinkle with a little rolled oats.

soft garlic & parsley wholewheat pull-apart rolls
Prepare the basic recipe, adding 2 minced cloves of garlic and 2 teaspoons chopped parsley to the flour with the softened butter.

variations

honey wheat rolls

see base recipe page 243

fruit & honey wheat rolls with oat topping
Prepare the basic recipe, adding 1 tablespoon each of currants, sultanas and cranberries to the flour with the orange juice. Just before baking, brush the tops of the rolls with a little beaten egg and sprinkle with a little rolled oats.

cinnamon & raisin honey wheat rolls
Prepare the basic recipe, adding 60 g (2 oz) raisins and 2 teaspoons cinnamon to the flour with the orange juice.

honey wheat rolls with anchovy butter
Prepare the basic recipe, and serve the rolls with halved radishes and anchovy butter on the side. Mix 100 g (4 oz) unsalted butter at room temperature with 4 finely chopped anchovy fillets and 2 tablespoons chopped fresh chives.

maple syrup wheat rolls
Prepare the basic recipe, replacing 2 tablespoons honey with maple syrup.

quick gluten-free and yeast-free rolls

see base recipe page 245

quick gluten-free rolls with basil
Prepare the basic recipe, adding 2 tablespoons chopped basil to the mixture with the flaxseed.

quick gluten-free rolls with sage
Prepare the basic recipe, adding 1 tablespoon dried sage to the mixture with the flaxseed.

quick gluten-free and yeast-free rolls with Parmesan
Prepare the basic recipe, adding 2 tablespoons finely grated Parmesan cheese to the mixture with the flaxseed.

quick gluten-free rolls with garlic & thyme
Prepare the basic recipe, adding 1 tablespoon garlic powder and 1 tablespoon dried thyme to the mixture with the flaxseed.

quick gluten-free rolls with poppy seeds
prepare the basic recipe, adding 1 tablespoon poppy seeds to the mixture with the flaxseed.

holiday breads

In this chapter, you will find breads from all
around the world, traditionally prepared at special
holiday times, and recipes that are ideal to be
served at those times.

hot cross buns

see variations page 272

These buns have a rich, golden dough, aromatic with spices and sweetened with dried fruit.

450 g (1 lb) white bread flour
50 g (2 oz) + 1 tsp sugar
2 cardomom pods, crushed
$^1/_2$ tsp ground ginger
$^1/_4$ tsp ground cloves
$^1/_4$ tsp freshly grated nutmeg
1 tsp salt

2 tsp active dry yeast
240 ml (8 fl oz) + 1 tbsp milk
100 g (4 oz) butter, softened
2 eggs, room temperature
140 g (5 oz) currants
40 g (1$^1/_2$ oz) sultanas
zest of 1 orange and 1 lemon

for the cross
1 egg, lightly beaten
65 g (2$^1/_4$ oz) plain flour

for the glaze
2 tbsp sugar, mixed with
  2 tbsp boiling water

Line 2 large baking sheets with baking paper. In the bowl of a free standing mixer with a dough hook attachment, add the flour, sugar and all the spices. Add the salt on one side, the yeast on the other. Make a well in the centre, and add the milk, butter and eggs. Mix on slow speed until a dough comes together, and knead for 5-8 minutes until the dough is soft, smooth and elastic. Add the currants, golden raisins, and orange and lemon zest, and mix for 1 minute. Transfer the dough to a large lightly oiled bowl and turn it around to coat it all over. Cover and place somewhere warm until doubled in size, up to 2 hours. Turn dough out onto a lightly floured work surface and knead for 1–2 minutes. Divide into 16 equal portions, and form each into a ball. Arrange on the baking sheets, 2.5 cm (1 in) apart, cover with lightly oiled cling film and leave for an hour to rise again. Preheat the oven to 200°C (400°F). Brush the buns with egg wash. Mix the flour with enough water to make a thick paste, spoon into a small-tipped piping bag, and pipe a cross in the middle of each bun. Bake for 20 minutes, until golden brown. Remove from the oven, transfer to a wire rack and brush with glaze. Serve warm, split, with plenty of butter.

Makes 16 buns

chocolate-walnut babka bread

see variations page 273

This indulgent treat is special enough to serve on any holiday morning.

285 g (10 oz) plain flour
60 g (2 oz) brown sugar
zest of 1 lemon
pinch of salt
1 tsp instant dry yeast
1 egg, room temperature, lightly beaten
6 tbsp warm water
85 g (3 oz) + 1 tbsp butter, room temperature

for the filling
100 g (4 oz) lightly toasted walnut halves
65 g (2$^1/_2$ oz) good-quality dark chocolate
85 g (3 oz) unsalted butter
30 g (1 oz) icing sugar, sieved
2 tbsp unsweetened cocoa powder, sieved
1 tbsp cinnamon
1 tbsp sugar

In a large bowl, mix the flour, sugar and lemon zest together. Add the salt on one side and the yeast on the other. Add the egg and water. Mix until a dough starts to form. Add in the butter, a little at a time, and knead for 5–8 minutes until smooth and elastic. Transfer the dough to a large, lightly oiled bowl and turn to coat it all over. Cover and refrigerate overnight. The next day, make the filling: Melt the chocolate and butter in a microwave. Stir in the icing sugar, cocoa powder, and cinnamon. Turn the dough out onto a lightly floured work surface, and roll out to a 38 x 28-cm (15 x 11-in) rectangle. Spread the filling over the dough, leaving a border of 1.9 cm (¾ in). Sprinkle with walnuts and sugar. With water, dampen a short edge of the dough, and tightly roll up. Turn the roll 90 degrees, with the seam underneath, and trim 1.5 cm (½ in) off each end. Cut in half lengthwise so that the inner ribbons of chocolate paste are exposed, and gently entwine the 2 pieces of dough together. Carefully into a buttered 900-g (2-lb) 23 x 13-cm (9 x 5-in) loaf pan. Cover, and put in a warm place for 90 minutes. Preheat the oven to 190°C (375°F). Bake for about 30 minutes, or until a toothpick inserted into the centre comes out clean. Cool on a wire rack.

Makes 1 loaf

bolo rei (portuguese twelfth night cake)

see variations page 274

This celebratory, brightly coloured bread is rich with candied fruit and nuts.

1 tsp + 100 g (4 oz) sugar, divided
80 ml (3 fl oz) warm whole milk
2 tsp active dry yeast
400 g (14 oz) + 2 tbsp plain flour
1 tsp salt
85 g (3 oz) mixed chopped candied fruit
30 g (1 oz) walnuts, coarsely chopped
30 g (1 oz) almonds, coarsely chopped

65 g (2½ oz) raisins, soaked in 1 tbsp port
zest of 1 lemon and 1 orange
100 g (4 oz) butter, melted and cooled
3 eggs, room temperature, lightly beaten
140 g (5 oz) mixed candied fruit
10 walnut halves
10 whole blanched almonds
2 tbsp sugar mixed with 2 tbsp boiling water

Line a large baking sheet with baking paper. Dissolve 1 teaspoon sugar in the milk, sprinkle the yeast over and leave for 10–15 minutes until frothy. In a large bowl, combine the flour and salt. Add 100 g (4 oz) sugar, chopped candied fruit, nuts, raisins and lemon and orange zest, and mix. Make a well in the centre, and add the yeast liquid, melted and cooled butter and eggs. Mix until a dough forms, and knead for 2–3 minutes. Transfer the dough to a large lightly oiled bowl and turn it to coat it all over. Cover and put in a warm place for 2 hours. Turn the dough out on to a lightly floured work surface, gently deflate the dough and form it into a wreath shape. Transfer to the baking sheet and decorate with candied fruit and nuts. Cover, and leave for 1 hour. Preheat the oven to 180°C (350°F) and bake for about 20 minutes, or until golden brown. Remove from the oven and cool on a wire rack. Brush with the sugar syrup glaze while warm.

Makes 1 cake

christmas-morning sugarplum bread

see variations page 275

Sugarplums are associated with Christmas because of 'The Night Before Christmas' poem and *The Nutcracker* ballet. The name signifies, among other things, everything sweet and delectable and lovely.

170 g (6 oz) brown sugar
100 g (4 oz) butter
2 tbsp golden syrup
1 tsp white sugar
300 ml (10 fl oz) warm milk

2 tsp instant dry yeast
450 g (1 lb) white bread flour
1 tsp salt
oil for greasing
1 tbsp cinnamon

340 g (12 oz) sugar
50 g (2 oz) chopped pecans
85 g (3 oz) maraschino
   cherries, quartered

Grease a 23-cm (9-in) fluted ring tin with a little oil. Make the glaze. In a medium pan, gently heat the brown sugar, butter and golden syrup together. Stir until the butter has melted and the sugar has dissolved. Set aside to cool.

Dissolve the sugar in the warm milk, sprinkle yeast over the top and leave for 10–15 minutes until frothy. In a large bowl, combine the flour and salt. Make a well in the centre, add the yeast liquid and work to a soft dough. If the mixture feels too dry, add a little extra water, and if it feels too wet, add a little extra flour. Turn out on to a lightly floured work surface and knead for about 10 minutes until it is soft, smooth and elastic. Combine the cinnamon and the sugar in a bowl. Turn the dough out on to a lightly floured work surface, form into a thick log and cut into about 32 pieces. Roll quickly into balls. Dip each ball in the cooled glaze and then roll in the cinnamon sugar. Layer the balls in the tin, leaving room on the bottom layer for the balls to expand as they rise. They should be close, but not touching. Sprinkle half the

pecans and cherries on top of the first layer. On each successive layer, place balls so that they overlap empty spaces underneath, and sprinkle the remaining pecans and cherries on as you go. When you have used up all the balls, pour any remaining glaze over the top and sprinkle on remaining cinnamon sugar. Cover and leave to rise at room temperature for about 1½ hours, until doubled in size. Preheat the oven to 170°C (325°F). Remove cover and bake for about 25–30 minutes, until browned. Leave to cool in the tin for 5 minutes. Invert bread on to a serving plate, being careful of the hot syrup and cool slightly before serving.

Makes 6 servings

german marzipan stollen

see variations page 276

A delicious Christmas bread, studded with candied and dried fruit.

1 tsp + 100 g (4 oz) sugar, divided	65 g (2¼ oz) sultanas
120 ml (4 fl oz) warm whole milk	65 g (2¼ oz) currants
2 tsp active dry yeast	65 g (2¼ oz) glacé cherries
310 g (11¼ oz) white bread flour	65 g (2¼ oz) chopped candied lemon peel
1 tsp cinnamon	zest of 1 orange
½ tsp salt	200 g (7 oz) marzipan
6 tbsp butter, softened	icing sugar
2 eggs, room temperature, lightly beaten	1 tbsp sliced almonds, toasted, for topping

Line a large baking sheet with baking paper. Dissolve 1 teaspoon sugar in the warm milk, sprinkle the yeast on top and leave for 10–15 minutes until frothy. In a large bowl, combine the flour, 100 g (4 oz) sugar, cinnamon, nutmeg and salt. Make a well in the centre, and add the yeast liquid, softened butter and eggs. Mix until a soft dough comes together. Add the raisins, currants, glacé cherries, lemon peel and orange zest, and knead for 5–8 minutes, until smooth and elastic. Transfer to a large lightly oiled bowl and turn it to coat it all over. Cover and put in a warm place for an hour or so, until doubled in size. Turn out on to a lightly floured work surface and gently deflate the dough. Press into an oblong shape about 25 x 20 cm (10 x 8 in). Roll the marzipan into a log about 23 cm (9 in) long and lay it down the centre of the dough. Roll the dough up and seal it well. Transfer the dough to the baking sheet with the seam underneath, loosely cover with cling film and put in a warm place for an hour to rise again. Preheat the oven to 150°C (300°F). Bake for around 35 minutes, or until golden brown. Cool on a wire rack, dust with icing sugar and sprinkle with almonds.

Makes 1 loaf

challah

see variations page 277

This delicious classic Jewish celebratory bread is traditionally served sliced and buttered on the Sabbath and festival days.

510 g (1 lb 2 oz) white bread flour
3 tbsp sugar
1 tsp salt
2 tsp instant dry yeast
2 eggs, room temperature, lightly beaten

40 g (1 1/2 oz) butter, softened
60 ml (2 fl oz) warm whole milk
180 ml (6 fl oz) warm water
beaten egg for brushing

Line a large baking sheet with baking paper. In the bowl of a stand mixer, combine the flour and sugar. Add the salt on one side and the yeast on the other, make a well in the centre and add the beaten eggs, butter and warm milk and water. Mix until a soft but not soggy dough forms. Using the dough hook attachment, knead for 5–8 minutes, until the dough starts to form a soft and smooth skin. Transfer the dough to a large lightly oiled bowl and turn to coat it all over. Put in a warm place for about 2–3 hours until doubled in size. Turn the dough out on to a lightly floured work surface, punch down and knead for 2–3 minutes, until smooth. Divide the dough into three equal portions, and roll each one into a log about 23 cm (9 in) long. Pinch the pieces together at one end, braid the dough from that end, pinch the other end together and tuck both ends under to neaten. Transfer to the baking sheet, brush with beaten egg and place inside an oiled plastic bag. Put in a warm place for an hour or so, until the loaf has doubled in size and springs back lightly when you press it with your finger. Preheat the oven to 200°C (400°F). Bake for 20–25 minutes, or until golden brown and the loaf sounds hollow when tapped on the bottom. Cool on a wire rack.

Makes 1 loaf

easter chocolate-nut danish

see variations page 278

This rich dough looks a bit like an iced cake, but conceals a delicious cinnamon, chocolate and almond filling.

double quantity of croissant dough
(see recipe page 60), rested overnight in
the fridge
225 g (8 oz) almonds, divided
50 g (2 oz) icing sugar
30 g (1 oz) unsweetened cocoa powder

1 tsp cinnamon
50 g (2 oz) unsalted butter + extra for greasing
1 egg white
60 g (2 oz) dark chocolate, chopped
1 egg yolk
2 tbsp whole milk

Generously butter the base and sides of a 23-cm (9-in) springform tin. Make the filling. Put three-quarters of the almonds into a food processor with the icing sugar, cocoa powder and cinnamon, and pulse a few times to combine. Add the butter and egg white, and pulse again until it becomes a paste. Fold in the chopped chocolate and set aside. Remove the dough from the fridge and divide it in half. Press one half into the base of the tin, spread the filling over the middle of the dough, leaving a 2.5-cm (1-in) border around the edge and cover with the remaining dough. Cover with cling film and put in a warm place for about an hour.

Preheat the oven to 180°C (350°F). In a small bowl, mix the egg yolk and milk together. Remove the cover and brush over the top of the dough. Sprinkle with the remainder of the sliced almonds and bake for about 50 minutes, until risen and golden brown. Leave to cool in the tin for 1 hour, then cool on a wire rack. Mix the icing sugar with a little water to make a runny icing, and drizzle it over the cake.

Makes 8 servings

moravian sugar cake

see variations page 279

This sweet Moravian treat is topped with a mixture of cinnamon, butter and brown sugar, and served on Easter morning.

1 tsp + 100 g (3½ oz) sugar, divided
120 ml (4 fl oz) warm water
4 tsp active dry yeast
2 tbsp powdered milk
1 tsp salt
120 ml (4 fl oz) water

60 ml (2 fl oz) whole milk
55 g (2 oz) potatoes, cooked, mashed, and cooled
115 g (4 oz) butter, melted and cooled, divided
2 eggs, room temperature, lightly beaten

375 g (13 oz) white bread flour
2 tablespoons cold butter for dotting + extra for greasing
200 g (7 oz) brown sugar
1 tsp cinnamon

Generously butter a large baking pan. In a large bowl, dissolve 1 teaspoon sugar in the warm water, sprinkle the yeast on top, and leave for 10–15 minutes until frothy. Add the remaining sugar, powdered milk, salt, water, whole milk, mashed potatoes, half the melted butter, eggs and a third of the flour. Beat with a wooden spoon, and add the remaining flour until you have a very soft and sticky dough. Transfer to a large lightly oiled bowl, dot with butter, cover and leave in a warm place for an hour or so, until doubled in size.

Turn the dough out onto a lightly floured work surface, gently deflate the dough and place in the baking pan. Cover and leave to rise for 30 minutes. Sprinkle with brown sugar and cinnamon. Punch your fingers into the dough, making indentations. Pour on the remaining melted butter, cover and leave for another 30 minutes. Preheat the oven to 190°C (375°F). Remove the cover and bake for 12–15 minutes, until golden brown. Cool on a wire rack and serve warm.

Makes 1 cake

hallowe'en irish barm brack

see variations page 280

This traditional Irish bread used to be baked at Hallowe'en with a ring, a coin and a thimble inside, signifying marriage, wealth and, strangely, a spinster!

1 tsp sugar, dissolved in 180 ml (6 fl oz) water	85 g (3 oz) brown sugar
1 tbsp active dry yeast	140 g (5 oz) sultanas
450 g (1 lb) plain flour	140 g (5 oz) raisins
1 tsp salt	140 g (5 oz) currants
1 tsp pumpkin pie spice	140 g (5 oz) dried cranberries
100 g (4 oz) butter, diced + extra for greasing	1 egg, room temperature, lightly beaten

Lightly butter two 450-g (1-lb) 20 x 10-cm (8 x 4-in) loaf tins. Sprinkle the yeast over the sugar–water mix and leave for 10–15 minutes until frothy. In a large bowl, combine the flour, salt and pumpkin pie spice. Cut in the butter until the mixture resembles fine breadcrumbs, and add the brown sugar and dried fruit. Make a well in the centre, and add the yeast liquid and beaten egg. Mix well, and turn the dough out on to a lightly floured work surface. Knead for 10 minutes, until smooth and elastic. Place the dough in a large lightly oiled bowl and turn to coat it. Cover and put in a warm place for an hour or so, or until doubled in size.

Preheat the oven to 180°C (350°F). Turn the dough out on to a lightly floured work surface and knead for 1–2 minutes. Divide the dough in half and shape to fit the two loaf tins. Place the tins in lightly greased plastic bags and leave until the dough rises above the sides of the tins. Remove the bags and bake in the oven for 50–60 minutes, until the bottom of the loaves sound hollow when tapped. Cool on a wire rack.

Makes 2 loaves

vanocka (czech christmas bread)

see variations page 281

This is a soft, intricately braided loaf, generously spiced with ginger and nutmeg.

500 g (1 lb 2 oz) white bread flour
55 g (2 oz) sugar
1 tsp salt
1½ envelopes (1 tbsp) active dry yeast
160 ml (5½ fl oz) warm whole milk
1 egg, room temperature
55 g (2 oz) butter, melted and cooled
1 tsp ground ginger
½ tsp ground nutmeg

zest of 1 lemon and 1 orange
55 g (2 oz) slivered blanched almonds
55 g (2 oz) raisins

for the topping
1 egg yolk beaten with 1 tbsp water,
   for egg wash
2 tbsp sliced almonds
icing sugar

In a large bowl, combine the flour, sugar and salt. Dissolve the yeast in the warm milk, and set aside for 5 minutes. Make a well in the centre of the flour and pour in the yeast liquid. Mix a little flour into the milk in the middle of the bowl to make a runny batter and set aside for 15-20 minutes. Add the egg, butter, ginger, nutmeg and lemon and orange zest. Mix to a firm dough, cover and put in a warm place for an hour or so, until doubled in size. Turn the dough out onto a lightly floured work surface, punch down and knead in the almonds and raisins. Cut the dough into eight equal portions. Roll each between your hands to form a rope about 45 cm (18 in) long. Braid five of the ropes, pinching them together at each end and place on the baking sheet. Braid the remaining three ropes and centre this braid on top of the fat braid. With wetted fingers, gently press the braids together, pinch the ends and press them under the ends of the fat braid. Leave to rise for an hour on a lined baking sheet, then brush with the egg wash, and sprinkle the sliced almonds over the top. Bake in the oven for about 50 minutes, until golden brown. Leave to cool on a wire rack and dust with icing sugar.

Makes 1 loaf

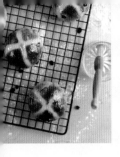

variations

hot cross buns

see base recipe page 259

chocolate chip & orange hot cross buns
Prepare the basic recipe, replacing the currants with 100 g (4 oz) chocolate chips and adding 2 teaspoons pure orange extract with the eggs.

cherry & macadamia-nut hot cross buns
Prepare the basic recipe, replacing the currants with dried cherries and the sultanas with 30 g (1 oz) chopped macadamia nuts.

cranberry & white chocolate chip buns
Prepare the basic recipe, replacing the currants with cranberries and the sultanas with 50 g (2 oz) white chocolate chips.

apricot & almond hot cross buns
Prepare the basic recipe, replacing the currants with chopped, dried ready-to-eat apricots and the sultanas with 40 g (1½ oz) sliced almonds.

variations

chocolate-walnut babka bread

see base recipe page 260

chocolate-pecan babka bread
Prepare the basic recipe, replacing the walnuts with chopped pecans.

chocolate-hazelnut babka bread
Prepare the basic recipe, replacing the walnuts with toasted and chopped hazelnuts.

mocha-walnut babka bread with kahlua
Prepare the basic recipe. Add 2 teaspoons instant coffee powder mixed with 2 teaspoons boiling water, and 1 tablespoon Kahlua to the filling.

variations

bolo rei (portuguese twelfth night cake)

see base recipe page 261

three kings bread
Prepare the basic recipe, omitting 2 of the eggs. Replace the plain flour with bread flour, and the candied fruit and nuts with 3 tablespoons glacé cherries. Form into a wreath shape and proceed as directed. Omit the glaze and mix 125 g (4½ oz) icing sugar with enough milk to make a fairly stiff icing. Spread it over the cooled bread.

panettone
Prepare the basic recipe, omitting 1 of the eggs and the nuts. Replace the plain flour with bread flour. Halve the amounts of candied fruit and dried fruit, and add 1 teaspoon vanilla extract and ½ teaspoon aniseed. Panettone is traditionally baked in a tall, cylindrical tin, so see what you can find to use with around 500 g (1 lb) capacity, such as a coffee tin. Cover and leave to rise. Bake as directed, but for 30 minutes. Omit glaze.

greek new year's bread
Prepare the basic recipe, omitting 2 eggs and replacing the plain flour with bread flour. Omit the candied fruit, dried fruit and nuts. After the first rising, punch down and roll into a rope about 75 cm (30 in) long. Coil it into a circle on a buttered baking sheet and insert a foil-wrapped coin inside, underneath, out of sight. Cover and rise again. Brush bread with egg white and water, and stick pine nuts around the top. Sprinkle with sugar and bake as directed, but for 30 minutes. Omit glaze.

christmas-morning sugarplum bread

see base recipe page 262

christmas-morning cranberry & walnut sugarplum bread
Prepare the basic recipe, replacing the cherries and pecans with cranberries and chopped walnuts.

christmas-morning apricot & almond sugarplum bread
Prepare the basic recipe, replacing the cherries and pecans with chopped, dried ready-to-eat apricots and sliced almonds.

christmas-morning apple & raisin sugarplum bread
Prepare the basic recipe, replacing the cherries and pecans with 1 peeled, cored and finely chopped apple and 85 g (3 oz) raisins.

christmas-morning chocolate chip sugarplum bread
Prepare the basic recipe, adding 75 g (2½ oz) dark chocolate chips with the cherries and pecans.

variations

german marzipan stollen

see base recipe page 264

glazed stollen wreath
Prepare the basic recipe. Roll the dough into a 50 x 20-cm (21 x 8-in) rectangle, and roll 340 g (12 oz) marzipan into a log 50 cm (21 in) long. Place it down the centre of the dough and roll the dough over the marzipan. Turn the dough over and lift on to the baking sheet so that the seam is underneath. Curl the dough around a buttered 12-cm (5-in) cake tin, brushing the ends with a little beaten egg and pinching them together to seal well. Leave to rise and bake as directed. Glaze with 65 g (2¼ oz) sieved icing sugar mixed with enough milk to make a runny icing, and drizzle it back and forth across the cooled stollen. Decorate the top with cranberries.

stollen with cranberries
Prepare the basic recipe, replacing the currants with dried cranberries.

mini stollen loaves
Prepare the basic recipe, dividing the dough and the marzipan into 6 equal portions. Roll the pieces of dough out into rectangles and the marzipan into logs 10 cm (4 in) long. Place the marzipan in the middle of the dough and proceed as directed. Bake for 25 minutes.

braided stollen
Prepare the basic recipe, omitting the marzipan. After the first rising, punch down and divide the dough into 3 equal portions. Pinch one end together, braid the dough to the other end, pinch that together also and tuck both ends under to neaten. Bake as directed.

variations

challah

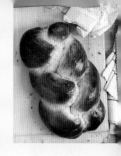

see base recipe page 265

glazed raisin challah
Prepare the basic recipe, adding 170 g (6 oz) raisins and 1 teaspoon cinnamon to the flour. Make a glaze with 125 g (4½ oz) sieved icing sugar mixed with enough milk to make a fairly stiff icing, and spread it over the cooled challah.

chocolate chip & banana challah
Prepare the basic recipe, adding 125 g (4½ oz) extra flour and 85 g (3 oz) dark chocolate chips to the flour, and 2 very ripe mashed bananas to the dough with the eggs and butter. If the dough still feels too sticky, add more flour until the consistency is right.

blueberry & white chocolate challah
Prepare the basic recipe, adding 170 g (6 oz) dried blueberries and 50 g (2 oz) white chocolate chips to the flour.

apple & cinnamon challah
Prepare the basic recipe. Add 2 teaspoons cinnamon, 1 teaspoon ground ginger and 1 peeled, cored and chopped apple to the flour.

variations

easter chocolate-nut danish

see base recipe page 266

easter mocha-nut danish
Prepare the basic recipe, adding 2 teaspoons instant coffee mixed with 2 teaspoons boiling water to the filling.

easter chocolate-orange danish
Prepare the basic recipe, adding 2 teaspoons pure orange extract to the filling.

easter chocolate danish with cranberries & amaretto
Prepare the basic recipe, adding 100 g (4 oz) dried cranberries and 2 tablespoons amaretto to the filling.

variations

moravian sugar cake

see base recipe page 267

sweet potato & cinnamon moravian sugar cake
Prepare the basic recipe, replacing the mashed potatoes with the same quantity of sweet potato puree, and the sugar with brown sugar. Add 1 teaspoon cinnamon.

moravian sugar cake with butterscotch sauce
Prepare the basic recipe. Melt 115 g (4 oz) butter over a gentle heat, add 4 tablespoons golden syrup, 300 g (10½ oz) brown sugar, 300 ml (10½ fl oz) whipping cream and 2 tablespoons lemon juice. Simmer for 5 minutes, cool and serve warm.

moravian sugar cake with lemon & blueberries
Prepare the basic recipe. Add 85 g (3 oz) dried blueberries and the grated rind of 1 lemon to the dough with the last lot of flour.

moravian sugar cake with crushed strawberry cream
Prepare the basic recipe. Warm 4 tablespoons strawberry preserves and add a large handful hulled and sliced strawberries. Cook for 3 minutes until the strawberries are slightly crushed and merging into the preserve. Cool. Lightly whip 240 ml (8 fl oz) double cream and 4 tablespoons sieved icing sugar together in a medium bowl, and lightly fold the strawberries into the cream; just a few turns will do it. Serve on the side with the sugar cake.

variations

hallowe'en irish barm brack

see base recipe page 268

maple-syrup irish barm brack
Prepare the basic recipe, omitting 2 tablespoons warm water and adding 2 tablespoons maple syrup with the egg. Brush the warm loaf with a little maple syrup to glaze.

hallowe'en irish barm brack with orange glaze
Prepare the basic recipe, omitting 2 tablespoons water. Add the zest of 2 oranges and 2 tablespoons freshly squeezed orange juice with the egg. Make a glaze by warming 85 g (3 oz) orange marmalade with 1 teaspoon water over a low heat until runny enough to brush over the warm loaf.

egg-free banana irish barm brack
Prepare the basic recipe, replacing the egg with 1 ripe mashed banana and 1 teaspoon ground flaxseed soaked in 3 tablespoons hot water for 5 minutes.

dairy-free hallowe'en irish barm brack
Prepare the basic recipe, replacing the butter with dairy-free margarine.

variations

vanocka (czech christmas bread)

see base recipe page 271

sweet potato vanocka
Prepare the basic recipe, adding an extra 125 g (4½ oz) bread flour, another 1 teaspoon cinnamon, and 100 g (3½ oz) sweet potato puree with the egg. If the dough still feels too sticky, add a little more flour until the consistency feels right.

pumpkin spice vanocka
Prepare the basic recipe, adding 2 teaspoons pumpkin spice to the flour.

cranberry & pecan vanocka
Prepare the basic recipe, replacing the raisins with dried cranberries and the almonds with chopped pecans.

index

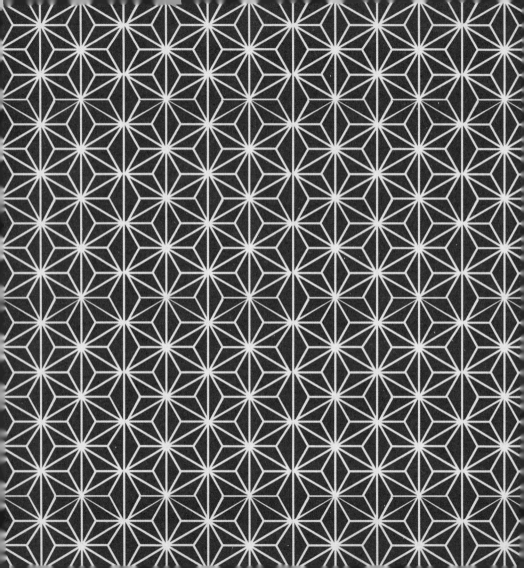